# SCRIPTING

## SOCIAL COMMUNICATION FOR ADOLESCENTS

Patty Mayo

Pattii Waldo

Thinking Publications
Eau Claire, Wisconsin

00   99   98   97   96   95   94        12   11   10   9   8   7   6

ISBN 0-930599-08-X

---

*Library of Congress Cataloging-in-Publication Data*
Mayo, Patty.
    Scripting : social communication for adolescents / Patty Mayo, Pattii Waldo. —2nd ed.
       p.  cm.
    Includes bibliographical references (p.   ).
    ISBN 0-930599-08-X (pbk.)
    1. Social skills—Study and teaching (Elementary).  2. Social skills—Study and teaching (Secondary).
3. Social interaction in adolescence—Study and teaching (Elementary).  4. Social interaction in adolescence—
Study and teaching (Secondary).  5. Role playing.
I. Waldo, Pattii.  II. Title.
HQ783.M37  1994
302'.14'07—dc20

94-27121
CIP

Cover Design: Robert T. Baker
Photographer: James H. Christoffersen
*Printed in the United States of America*

*A Division of McKinley Companies, Inc.*

424 Galloway Street
Eau Claire, WI 54703

715-832-2488
FAX 715-832-9082

# Table of Contents

Preface ................................................................................................................. v

Acknowledgments ................................................................................................ vii

**Chapter 1: Introduction** ................................................................................... 1

    Overview .......................................................................................................... 1

    How to Use ....................................................................................................... 4

**Chapter 2: Skill-Step Presentation** .................................................................. 9

**Follow-Up Activities** ......................................................................................... 14

**Glossary** ............................................................................................................... 18

**References** ........................................................................................................... 19

**Social Communication Skills Scripts**

    *Introductory Skills*

        Skill 1: Eye Contact ........................................................................... 21

        Skill 2: Manners ................................................................................. 26

        Skill 3: Volume .................................................................................. 31

        Skill 4: Choosing the Right Time and Place ...................................... 36

        Skill 5: Tone of Voice ........................................................................ 40

        Skill 6: Getting to the Point .............................................................. 44

        Skill 7: Staying on Topic .................................................................... 49

        Skill 8: Listening ................................................................................ 54

        Skill 9: Starting and Ending a Conversation ...................................... 59

        Skill 10: Proximity ............................................................................ 64

        Skill 11: Formal/Informal Language .................................................. 69

        Skill 12: Making a Good Impression ................................................. 75

    *General Interaction Skills*

        Skill 13: Interrupting ......................................................................... 79

        Skill 14: Planning What to Say .......................................................... 83

        Skill 15: Receiving a Compliment ..................................................... 88

        Skill 16: Giving a Compliment .......................................................... 92

        Skill 17: Saying Thank You ............................................................... 96

        Skill 18: Introducing Yourself ........................................................... 101

        Skill 19: Introducing Others ............................................................. 106

        Skill 20: Offering Help ...................................................................... 111

        Skill 21: Asking for Help ................................................................... 116

        Skill 22: Asking Permission .............................................................. 121

        Skill 23: Accepting No ...................................................................... 126

*General Interaction Skills—Continued*

Skill 24: Making an Apology.................................................................131

Skill 25: Stating an Opinion...............................................................137

Skill 26: Agreeing/Disagreeing...........................................................141

Skill 27: Convincing Others...............................................................146

Skill 28: Giving Information..............................................................151

Skill 29: Dealing with Contradictions................................................157

*Peer Interaction Skills*

Skill 30: Starting a Friendship...........................................................162

Skill 31: Giving Emotional Support....................................................168

Skill 32: Attending and Ignoring.......................................................172

Skill 33: Responding to Teasing.........................................................178

Skill 34: Peer Pressure.....................................................................183

Skill 35: Joining In.........................................................................189

Skill 36: Being Left Out...................................................................193

*Conflict Management Skills*

Skill 37: Being Assertive..................................................................198

Skill 38: Making a Complaint............................................................203

Skill 39: Receiving a Complaint.........................................................208

Skill 40: Giving Negative Feedback....................................................213

Skill 41: Accepting Negative Feedback................................................218

Skill 42: Dealing with a False Accusation.............................................223

Skill 43: Making an Accusation..........................................................228

Skill 44: Compromising/Negotiating...................................................233

Skill 45: Accepting Consequences.......................................................238

*Emotional Expression Skills*

Skill 46: Expressing Feelings.............................................................242

Skill 47: Expressing Anger................................................................247

Skill 48: Dealing with Embarrassment.................................................252

Skill 49: Coping with Fear................................................................257

Skill 50: Expressing "Safe" Humor.....................................................263

Skill 51: Accepting "Safe" Humor......................................................268

Skill 52: Dealing with Failure............................................................273

Skill 53: Expressing Affection...........................................................278

# Preface

*Scripting: Social Communication for Adolescents* was developed to fill a need in our classrooms, that is, to help our students develop social communication skills that would allow them to function at school, at home, and in the community. Our professional backgrounds include speech-language pathology (Patty Mayo) and emotional/behavioral disabilities (Pattii Waldo). At the time of writing, we are both teaching in a junior high school and sharing students who need social communication skill training between our classrooms. Our team efforts have been paying off as colleagues observe and comment on positive changes in our students. The students have felt better about themselves after participating in *Scripting* activities, and parents have noticed changes at home.

The behavioral changes in our students have inspired us to share our ideas with you. Advancement of any discipline occurs only when colleagues share their ideas and methods. We would like to share *Scripting: Social Communication for Adolescents* because it fills a need within special and general education as well as counseling programs. At the present time, a variety of resources focus on teaching social skills through a skill-step approach (Goldstein, Sprafkin, Gershaw, and Klein, 1980; McGinnis, Goldstein, Sprafkin, and Gershaw, 1984). However, there are very few programs available offering alternate activities and materials.

*Scripting: Social Communication for Adolescents* integrates the skill-step approach with a scripting technique. The program is used with young people at the secondary level who have at least minimal reading skills. *Scripting* is written at a fifth grade reading level (Dale-Chall readability formula); this permits the program to be used with students who have a wide range of abilities. *Scripting* provides structured activities suitable for those students displaying attention deficits or self-control problems.

Teachers of young people with disabilities have struggled along with their students as they try to pronounce a troublesome word or try to remember factual information. For the student who has academic problems, the struggle ends each day when he or she leaves the school. The student with social disabilities must always struggles; there is always a social situation that must be handled. Without adequate training, youth with social disabilities face a world of loneliness and isolation.

It is apparent from the numbers of young people with social disabilities that schools and other agencies designed to promote child development must direct their attention toward the dual goal of increasing academic and social competence. Only by providing direct instruction to meet these needs will educators help to lessen the social struggle of some youth.

# ACKNOWLEDGMENTS

To Lisa and Josh for their patience,

to Mike and Ron for their support,

to Laurie for her willingness to help and her hours of work,

to Nancy for her expertise,

and to all our students from whom we have learned so much,

***THANK YOU!***

# Chapter 1 Introduction

## Overview

*The bell rings. The clamor from the hall quiets as lockers close and students enter their classroom. Ms. Rose begins to enter the attendance in her record book. As she marks absences, she records a "mental" attendance for those students of special concern.*

*Slumped behind Lucinda is Passive Patty. Over in the corner is Unusual Martin. The students have already moved their desks away from him, creating a barrier. Suddenly, Ms. Rose notices how quiet the room is. She feels relief when she realizes that Hurricane Harry is absent. Ms. Rose replaces her record book in the desk and begins the lesson for the day. She is interrupted with the slam of the classroom door and a loud, "I'm sorry, Ms. Rose. I overslept." Hurricane Harry had arrived.*

Practically every classroom has students who are different and who just do not seem to fit in with the other students. These students are easily identified by peers and teachers alike. For a variety of reasons, these young people who are socially different are isolated from their peers either because of what they do or do not do. This isolation can continue throughout a lifetime, creating much unhappiness for the person who is socially different. Research indicates that individuals who are socially different are maladjusted in school, have higher delinquency rates, and are at high risk for adjustment problems as adults (McGinnis, Goldstein, Sprafkin, and Gershaw, 1984).

The Passive Patties, the Unusual Martins, and Hurricane Harries of the world represent three distinct groups of socially different individuals. The term *socially different* describes those individuals who are unable to maintain social acceptance by peers and adults. In Ms. Rose's classroom, Unusual Martin might be described as having a deficit in social skills. He may not have appropriate eye contact or know how to open and close conversations, for example. Gresham (1981) describes the Passive Patties as having a performance deficit. In other words, Passive Patties have the appropriate social skills in their repertoire, but for a variety of reasons (e.g., lack of practice, not being rewarded for the behavior) they do not use them. Hurricane Harries whirl through their lives in an uncontrolled manner. This lack of inner control prohibits them from displaying appropriate social skills. Gresham (1981) describes these individuals as having self-control deficits. Further, Elliott and Gresham (1991) have conceptualized five reasons for social skill deficit:

1. a lack of knowledge;

2. a lack of practice or feedback;

3. a lack of cues or opportunities;

4. a lack of reinforcement; and

5. the presence of interfering behaviors.

Emphasis is being placed on both the social ability and the academic ability of the young person with exceptional needs (Alley and Deshler, 1979; Elliott and Gresham, 1991; Gresham, 1984; Nippold, 1994; Schumaker and Hazel, 1984a, 1984b). If students do not socially to cope with the demands of the regular classroom, current practice suggests that they be taught specific social skills that will enhance their ability to achieve. The acquisition of these skills will not only help to ensure success in the classroom, but it will also help to establish social competence in other areas of the students' lives.

Identification of students requiring social skills training is not difficult. Students and instructors alike seem to categorize these individuals. The fictional characters at the beginning of this chapter were used to promote mental images of students the readers may know. For most educators, students in the categories described by Gresham (1981) and Elliott and Gresham (1991) are a familiar group.

Although most children with social differences can be identified through observation, providing them with appropriate programming may be more difficult. At one time, it was assumed that mainstreaming children with disabilities would promote social interaction, social acceptance, and modeling (Gresham, 1984). However, for many children who have disabilities, the opposite appears true. Many children who are mainstreamed are poorly accepted or are totally rejected by their peers in regular classes (Ballard, Corman, Gollieb, and Kaufman, 1977). Social interaction for mainstreamed children is minimal at best (Allen, Benning, and Drummond, 1972). In addition, children placed in a mainstreamed setting do not always appear to benefit socially through incidental social learning.

The need for specific social skill programs is evident for those students demonstrating social differences. A variety of approaches have been used. Madden and Slavin (1983) describe six methods for social skill instruction. These methods include coaching, teaching the skills, providing feedback, modeling, using behavior modification, and learning cooperatively. A direct instruction program involves modeling, role playing, reinforcing behavior, and initiating by peers (Strain, Odom, and McConnell, 1984).

McGinnis et al. (1984) and Goldstein, Sprafkin, Gershaw, and Klein (1980) advocate teaching social behaviors through a structured learning approach. The *structured learning approach* is described by McGinnis et al. (1984) as "a psychoeducational intervention designed to teach the skill deficient child prosocial behaviors and to facilitate the actual use of these alternatives" (p. 8). Structured learning is composed of four training components: modeling, role playing, performance feedback, and transfer of training.

## Description of *Scripting: Social Communication for Adolescents*

*Scripting: Social Communication for Adolescents* was originally developed within a public school program for adolescents with behavioral disorders. Many of the adolescents experienced impulsive behavior which prohibited them from benefiting from less structured role-playing experiences. These students read through and discussed the scripts. Following the script reading, they learned the skill steps, practiced the skill in a role-playing situation, and finally developed their own scripts utilizing the skill within personal situations. From the time the scripts were first developed, *Scripting* has been used successfully with students who have learning disabilities, language disabilities, cognitive impairments, and by those general education students requiring social skill training from ages twelve to sixteen.

*Scripting* presents one element of a social skills program. It is designed to be used with individuals who fit any of the groups of socially different persons described by Gresham (1981) and Elliott and Gresham (1991). The scripts provide a structured, specific approach in which the students have the opportunity to view the skill enacted appropriately and inappropriately. Although a variety of methods are available to facilitate social skill practice, *Scripting* follows the structured learning approach as advocated by McGinnis et al. (1984) and by Goldstein et al. (1980). The activities, the situations, and the scripts form the basis for specific skill units. Many of the situations are selected from real-life experiences of adolescents in a variety of environments (i.e., home, school, and community). The situations provided in *Scripting* can be utilized for skill practice. Both Scripts, A and B, can be used to introduce a skill or to reinforce use of the skill during role-playing experiences.

### Skill Steps

Skill steps are an important aspect of a social skills program. When skills have been identified for teaching, they must be broken down into specific steps which lead to the completion of the skill. The skill-step approach is similar to a task analysis. The target skill is identified and then broken down into "teachable units" of behavior. The skill steps are developed based upon students' needs. Some students will require a greater number of steps, while others will require fewer (see the example in Table 1.1). *Scripting* does not provide skill steps because a variety of resources already provide numerous skills divided into steps (Goldstein et al., 1980; Hazel, Schumaker, Sherman, and Sheldon-Wildgen, 1980; McGinnis et al., 1984; Stephans, 1978) and each group of students requires individualized skill steps. When developing a complete social skills program, *Scripting* should be used in conjunction with another

**Table 1.1    Skill Steps Planning**

Mr. Graham was planning for his social communication class. Students were learning how to use formal language when beginning a conversation. He developed the following skill steps:

1. Greet the person by using their name.

2. Listen for a reply.

3. Have a topic in mind to begin a conversation (e.g., your current job, a hobby).

During class the next day, Mr. Graham discovered through discussion with students that his skill steps were too general. The students did not know enough about formal language to greet another person. Mr. Graham expanded the skill steps to include:

1. Look at the person.

2. Say "Hello."

3. When greeting the other person, use "Mr.," "Mrs.," or "Ms." with their last name.

4. Give your name.

5. Give one fact about yourself.

6. Listen for a reply.

program featuring skill steps (Goldstein et al., 1980; McGinnis et al., 1984). The scripts were not written to include all skill steps but rather to focus on the principle of the skill.

## How to Use

### Skill Activities/Discussions

The skills in *Scripting* are introduced through an activity that is motivating to the students. Introductory activities are provided in *Scripting* through the Skill Activities/Discussions section of each unit. Once the skill is introduced, the skill steps are presented to the students. A variety of methods can be enlisted to teach the students the skill steps. The students can discuss each step. They can compare the steps with other skills previously learned or they can sequence the steps in inappropriate order. Refer to Chapter 2 of *Scripting* for an example of skill-step presentation.

## Scripts

Once the steps are learned, one of the scripts can be read. The explanation of each scene helps students choose the parts they prefer, and also allows students to be oriented to the scene. In special cases, such as with students who do not read well or with students who have participation problems, the educator may want to chose the parts for the students. Each part has been assigned a name. If the students want to personalize their part, they may choose to cross out the fictional name and write in their own. If additional practice is necessary, the students may enjoy creating their own fictional names. This technique helps to break the monotony of rereading the script.

The scripts in *Scripting* are reproducible. Ideally, each student should receive a script, because when all students have a script, the educator can provide for individual differences among students. For students who experience problems with staying on task, color-coding of the student's part might be helpful. The educator can also walk among the students as they are reading the scripts and point to the line that the class is reading. For those who have problems reading, a built-in assignment for each unit can be to practice the skill during a study period or at home. Through this extra practice, the students can familiarize themselves with the scripts before reading them in class. Not all scripts demand characters to speak extensively. Several scripts designate characters who are needed, but who have no lines. Numerous scripts have characters with only one or two lines that could be rehearsed and memorized, rather than read.

The scripts can be used by large or small groups. In a large group, parts can be given to some of the class members while others listen as observers. Additional parts, such as the part of the narrator, who reads all of the information in the brackets, can be created. With large groups, those students who are observing can be given special instructions, such as "listen for the skill steps" or "identify how the problem in this situation was solved." In most cases, the scripts involve three or four characters. However, in groups that have fewer students than characters in the script, students can take more than one part. Students can be motivated to play more than one character by instructing them to change their voices or to act differently for each character. In some scripts, characters can be combined. For example, if there is more that one friend in the script, one student can read both parts. The educator will, of course, have read the scripts ahead of time to learn which parts can be combined.

Two scripts are provided in each skill unit. Script A illustrates the correct performance of the skill. The utilization of Script A provides an opportunity for the students to practice the skill being used appropriately. Students can suggest other situations in which this skill can be used. Script A reinforces the skill steps in a practical situation and prepares students for role playing in related, but different, situations.

Script B demonstrates the skill being used inappropriately. Depending on the needs of the group, one or both scripts may be chosen for use within the skill unit. Students may benefit from reading through Script B because they often do not see their mistakes when attempting to use the skill outside of the classroom. After reading Script B, students are encouraged to discuss the skill steps that were not followed. They can suggest more appropriate ways of reacting to the situation in the script. Or they can discuss times when the same situation happened to them. Whatever the method used, after reading Script B the objective should be to discuss what went wrong in the script and what would have happened if the skill had been demonstrated appropriately.

## Alternative Settings

Three alternative settings are presented in the Situations section of each skill unit—one from a home setting, one from a school setting, and one from a community setting. These three environments were chosen:

1. To illustrate the relevance of the skill within the students' lives;

2. To promote transfer of the skill from the classroom into other environments; and

3. To increase the students' experiences with the skill.

The situations can be utilized within the skill activities as suggested in the Skill Activities/Discussions portion of each unit. Or the situations can be used for role playing after the scripts have been read.

## Follow-Up Activities

The Skill Activities/Discussions sections were designed to include both introductory and follow-up activities for each skill unit. The activities and the discussions help to motivate students who had previously failed to see the relevance of such learning. The activities and the discussions allow educators to indicate important features of each skill which are not apparent within the skill steps or the scripts.

Follow-up activity sheets are provided for homework assignments. According to Goldstein et al. (1980) and McGinnis et al. (1984), homework assignments help to promote skill transfer and generalization. After the students have demonstrated an understanding of the skill through discussions, script reading, and role playing, homework assignments should be given. Three follow-up activity sheets have been provided on pages 15–17. The choice of sheets depends on the student and the experiences that the educator desires the student to have. On all three study sheets, students have the opportunity to practice the skill in their own environment. Skill practice outside of the classroom should be encouraged.

## Conducting a Skill Unit

Each skill unit should take approximately five days of daily meetings of 30–45 minutes in length. The length of the skill unit can be adjusted based on students' needs and abilities. The five days could be broken into segments such as the following:

Day One: Introduce the skill.

Day Two: Present the skill steps.

Day Three: Present the scripts.

Day Four: Role play the skill, provide a homework assignment, and critique the role playing.

Day Five: Conduct concluding discussions, and review the homework experiences.

Choosing the skills to be taught can be accomplished through a variety of methods. Goldstein et al. (1980) and McGinnis et al. (1984) provide informal checklists which will help educators select the skills to teach. *SSS: Social Skill Strategies (Book A* and *Book B)* (Gajewski and Mayo, 1989a, 1989b) provide behavioral rating scales and checklists; one of which is a self-rating scale and another that is completed by significant others. Skill selection can also be based on daily observations of students' social abilities and on reports from others who interact with the student (e.g., parents, peers). Once the skills are selected, students' motivation can be increased by providing them with the opportunity to select the order in which the skills are presented.

Skill sequence should be given some consideration when choosing skills. Social abilities which are more basic, such as greeting someone or starting a conversation, should be studied first. The more complex skills, such as handling peer pressure or convincing others, should be taught after the students have learned the fundamental skills. In *Scripting*, the first twelve skills are basic to nearly all other skills taught. They should be constantly reinforced throughout the skill-training program. Such skills as giving eye contact, listening, starting and ending a conversation, and proximity are only a few of the skills to be emphasized. Maintaining student motivation within the social skills program is crucial to the success of the instruction. Throughout the instructional sessions, skill activities should be relevant to the students' experiences, needs, and interests. *Scripting* provides a variety of situations and scripts designed to match the daily life experiences of adolescents. The situations and scripts are based on home and family life, school, peers, community awareness, and employment. Encouraging the students to share their own experiences will help to make the skill units more interesting and relevant. Sharing personal experiences also helps to identify cultural and regional differences for each skill. Throughout the units, the use of humor helps to keep students on task. Laughing at the humor in some scripts or inventing silly character names helps students maintain their motivation.

Other motivation enhancers include field trips during which students practice their skills. Going to business places for tours, going out to eat, or visiting other places of interest provides opportunities for skill practice. These trips can be planned ahead of time and based upon completion of group goals. The inclusion of skilled peers is often helpful to the social skills class. Unpopular students often associate with other unpopular students making it difficult for them to gain the skills necessary to interact with socially skilled students (Bullock, 1988). The addition of skilled peers helps the students with social differences acquaint themselves with others outside of their usual circle of friends. Also, peers may provide positive modeling for the target students. Peers enjoy the activities because they are different from typical academic activities.

In many programs, a specific "social skills class" is not always available. However, social skills training still can, and should be, integrated into the student's day. *Scripting* can be used to enhance reading, English, and language arts classes. The real-life situations provide students with opportunities to respond orally or through written expression. Students can improve their reading by practicing fluency and expression. The creative educator will integrate *Scripting* into a variety of classroom experiences.

## Summary

*Scripting: Social Communication for Adolescents* represents a segment of a complete social skills program. The scripts can be used with a variety of adolescents who are socially different. *Scripting* provides a structured approach which is directed toward the relevant environments of the adolescent's life. The scripts, the situations, and the activities help to promote a unit approach to teaching social skills. Providing opportunities to learn appropriate behaviors will help to encourage a sense of self-satisfaction, accomplishment, and social-skill competence for individuals with social differences.

# Chapter 2 — Skill-Step Presentation

*Why don't you look where you're going, you jerk!*

*You're such a nerd!*

*Here comes good old Creepy Crawler. Hey, Creepy, why don't you crawl back under a rock where you belong?*

*Ms. Rose just shook her head as she walked down the crowded hall to her room. This year, the negative comments were really getting bad. The students just didn't seem to know how to be nice to one another. She decided to do something about the situation.*

## Step 1: Identification of the Problem

Ms. Rose didn't like the way students treated each other. Their comments were negative criticism.

## Step 2: Identification of the Skill

The students Ms. Rose observed either did not know how to compliment each other (skill deficit) or they did not use positive comments with their peers, even though this skill was within their repertoire (performance deficit). Ms. Rose decided to teach the skill of *giving compliments*.

## Step 3: Introduction of the Skill

Each student who entered Ms. Rose's room read the following instructions on the board: *Write down something nice about a person in this room.* When the students had finished their assignments, the papers were collected.

The students looked around the room to figure out who the statements were directed at, as Ms. Rose read them aloud. There was an assortment of comments, such as "Like your hair," and "You have pretty eyes." A few mentioned a person's qualities, such as "You have a nice personality." But a surprising number of the "compliments" were actually put-downs. One student wrote, "The haircut you got this time is a lot better than the last one you got."

When Ms. Rose had finished, the room was unusually quiet. Ms. Rose asked, "Well, what did you think of the comments?"

An outspoken young lady answered, "Ms. Rose, some of those comments were okay, but a lot of them were sort of putting the person down."

"That's a good point," replied Ms. Rose. "In fact, that's the point of this whole discussion. I've been hearing too many put-downs lately and not enough compliments. As a result, we will be studying how to give compliments within our Speech and Drama unit."

## Step 4: Skill Presentation

According to Ms. Rose's plan, she would teach her students the skill steps for giving compliments. To develop the steps, Ms. Rose considered the social needs of her students. From previous experiences, she knew that most students in her classes were socially adept with fundamental skills such as *eye contact* and *volume*. After considering the skill level of her students, she developed the following steps:

1. Decide if a compliment is necessary.
   Compliment rule: Ask yourself, "Did the person do something that you really liked?"

2. Choose the right time and place. Usually, a compliment is given right after someone has done something that you really like.

3. Compliment the person.

4. Give the reason for the compliment.

5. Listen for a response.

6. Continue with a conversation or close the conversation smoothly.

During class on the second day of the unit, Ms. Rose presented the skill steps. She decided to present the steps to the whole class and to discuss each one. After the presentation, she wanted the class to break into groups of two. The students, while in their groups, were to teach each other the skill steps by memory.

When the students learned the steps, Ms. Rose tested the class's recall. She presented a situation that required one person to compliment another. Through a discussion, the students described how they would give the compliment.

## Step 5: Scripting

Once the students understood the skill steps, the scripts from *Scripting* were presented to the class. Ms. Rose chose to present Script A first. The students selected parts and read the script. For those students who did not have a part, Ms. Rose suggested that they listen and decide if the skill was demonstrated correctly or incorrectly. Script B presented a situation in which a compliment given inappropriately. The students quickly identified which skill steps were missing from the script and why the compliment was considered inappropriate. Throughout the class discussions of Script A and Script B, Ms. Rose encouraged all students to share their own experiences of complimenting each other and receiving inappropriate compliments..

## Step 6: Skill Modeling

A situation that required a compliment was written on the board. Ms. Rose asked for a volunteer. She explained that she and the volunteer were going to role play giving a compliment by following all of the skill steps for the situation given. Initially, Ms. Rose rehearsed the skill steps with the volunteer before role playing for the class. After the role play was enacted and discussed, the students broke into groups of two. They were given three situations to practice. While the students practiced, Ms. Rose visited each group, making comments, and reinforcing each group's efforts.

## Step 7: Skill Role Play

By the end of the class, all of the students had the opportunity to practice the skill of *giving compliments* in a variety of situations. Ms. Rose gave the assignment for each student to write down their own situations in which a compliment was necessary. During the next class period, they would present their situation to the class through a role play.

As the students presented their plays, Ms. Rose made positive comments. After the presentations, she reinforced the skill steps by mentioning which steps were included.

## Step 8: Homework

Ms. Rose was pleased with her students' progress. In the classroom, the students did a nice job of complimenting each other. The class was given a homework assignment: They were to practice giving a compliment to a friend. They had to write: a) the skill steps; b) to whom the compliment was given; and c) in what situation. The person receiving the compliment was asked to sign the homework sheet. In addition to this practice, Ms. Rose also asked the students to keep a "compliment diary" for one week. The students were to record the times when they gave a compliment. Ms. Rose discussed the diary each day with the students.

## Step 9: Concluding Activities

The students entered the class on Friday to find a colorful assortment of boxes, ribbons, and wrapping paper. Ms. Rose stated that a compliment can be one of the best gifts to give. She asked each classmate to choose a name from a hat. When each student had the name of another classmate, Ms. Rose asked them to give a compliment in writing to the person they had drawn. After the compliment was written, the students could wrap it as a present.

## Step 10: Follow-Up Activities

During the weeks after the unit was presented, Ms. Rose was careful to recognize those students who complimented another person appropriately. She occasionally structured situations within the context of the class to provide opportunities for continued practice of this skill.

## Summary

The ten steps presented in developing a skill unit are an example. This unit was simplified and did not account for unexpected situations that would be specific to each class. Solutions to these situations depend on the educator's individual creativity. Providing additional scripting and modeling examples, or developing other strategies for students, may be necessary during any skill unit. Adding skill steps may be a solution, although the number should be kept small (i.e., less than ten) (McGinnis, Personal Communication, 1986). The educator must be prepared to provide for modification.

Users of *Scripting* may face skepticism by adolescents and educators who are familiar with the skill-training process. For students who are hesitant to try social skills training, a gradual introduction to the training process can be accomplished by involving the student in group activities designed to facilitate communication with other students. As adolescents begin to relax with their peers, the actual training program can begin. Extrinsic reinforcement can be provided for hesitant students and can be done in several ways. During the unit, the educator could provide adolescents with positive comments when they are deserved. Students with self-control problems can be encouraged to participate by providing a refreshment period at the end of each class, contingent upon their behavior and assignment completion. In more academic situations, grades can be given for homework and for role plays. If grades are given, the educator must make certain the student can perform the skill before the skill is critiqued and graded.

Because students often do homework assignments with their parents, educators should inform parents of the purpose of social skills training. If an informal meeting with the parents is not possible, an explanatory letter can be sent home. Whatever the method of communication, educators should solicit parental support. When parents also lack social skills, or when they are unsupportive, the students can practice new skills with a teacher, a friend, or another adult outside of the classroom.

The *Scripting* program, when combined with other activities, can shape a comprehensive social skills program. *Scripting: Social Communication for Adolescents* provides students with opportunities to view skills appropriately and inappropriately. From activities, discussions, role playing, and actual practice, students have experiences that prepare them for social communication in their daily lives.

 **ollow-Up Activities**

**Activity 1:** The *Follow-Up Activity 1* sheet could be completed by students as a homework assignment. It will promote transfer of each social communication skill taught because it asks the students to role play one of three situations with a parent or guardian. This activity sheet can be used with any of the social communication skills. Before the students take it home, add the following items to the sheets:

1. the current date

2. the student's name

3. the social communication skill

4. the skill steps

5. the due date

6. the three situations

7. your signature

If any students cannot role play with a parent or guardian, allow practice with another mutually agreed upon adult or sibling.

**Activity 2:** The *Follow-Up Activity 2* sheet could be used after reading Script A or Script B from any of the 53 units. It can be completed by students individually or as a group.

**Activity 3:** The *Follow-Up Activity 3* sheet can be used after students have read any Script B which portrays incorrect use of a social communication skill. As a group, have the students decide at what point in the script they should begin to rewrite the characters' lines. Instruct the students to create a new ending to the script from that point on so that it portrays correct use of the skill.

## Follow-Up Activity 1

Date: _____

**Dear Parent or Guardian of** _____ :

This week, we are learning about the social communication skill:

_____

This skill can be broken down into the following skill steps:

1.

2.

3.

4.

5.

6.

Please role play (practice) one of the three situations listed below with your son/daughter. Make certain that all the skill steps listed are followed. After completing the role play, sign your name on this sheet.

This activity sheet needs to be returned for our class meeting on _____.

**Situations:**

1.

2.

3.

By practicing this social communication skill at home, your child will be more likely to use the skill outside of the classroom setting.

Thank you for your assistance.

Sincerely,

_____

*Educator*

_____

*Parent/Guardian Signature*

# Follow-Up Activity 2

Date: _____

Name(s): _____

**Directions:** After reading one of the scripts, answer the following questions.

1. Name the social communication skill that was portrayed in this script.

   _____

2. How would you define this social communication skill?

   _____

   _____

3. Identify the character(s) in the script who dealt with the social communication skill.

   _____

4. Did the character(s) demonstrate correct or incorrect use of the social communication skill?
   (Explain why.)

   _____

   _____

5. How can developing and using this social communication skill help you?

   At home: _____

   _____

   At school: _____

   _____

   In the community: _____

   _____

6. Describe a time when you faced a social communication situation needing this skill. Tell whether
   you correctly or incorrectly followed the skill steps. Also, tell why you did or didn't follow the
   skill steps.

   _____

   _____

# Follow-Up Activity 3

Date: _____

Name(s): _____

**Social Communication Skill:** _____

**Directions:** Using the same characters, rewrite Script B so that it portrays correct use of the skill. Begin at the point where the skill first breaks down.

_____ : _____
                 _____

_____ : _____
                 _____

_____ : _____
                 _____

_____ : _____
                 _____

_____ : _____
                 _____

_____ : _____
                 _____

_____ : _____
                 _____

_____ : _____
                 _____

# Glossary

**MODELING.** Providing an example of social behavior which others try to duplicate.

**PERFORMANCE FEEDBACK.** Corrective criticism and positive comments given after a role play in which a social skill has been practiced.

**ROLE PLAY.** Individuals acting out a situation in which a specific social skill is being practiced.

**SCRIPTING.** Individuals practicing and discussing a specific social skill by reading through a script which features that skill.

**SKILL.** A particular social ability which is necessary for dealing with social situations found in daily life.

**SKILL GENERALIZATION.** Using a specific skill appropriately in a variety of novel situations outside of the original learning environment.

**SKILL PRACTICE.** Rehearsal of a social skill though role-play experiences.

**SKILL SEQUENCE.** The hierarchy established for social skills from beginning skills through advanced skills (e.g., eye contact is taught before conflict negotiation).

**SKILL STEPS.** The division of a specific social skill into sequential parts.

**SKILL TRANSFER.** Prior learning of a specific social skill which facilitates learning a similar skill.

**SKILL UNIT.** An organized plan for teaching a particular skill involving introductory and concluding activities, discussions, skill practice, modeling, scripting, and homework.

**STRUCTURED LEARNING APPROACH.** A four-step approach to teaching social skills, as advocated by Goldstein et al. (1980) and McGinnis et al. (1984), comprised of modeling, role playing, performance feedback, and transfer experiences.

# References

Allen, K., Benning, P., and Drummond, T. (1972). Integration of normal and handicapped children in behavior modification preschool: A case study. In G. Sumb (Ed.), *Behavior analysis and education*. Lawrence, KS: University of Kansas Press.

Alley, G., and Deshler, D. (1979). *Teaching the learning disabled adolescent: Strategies and methods*. Denver, CO: Love Publishing Company.

Ballard, M., Corman, L., Gollieb, J., and Kaufman, M. (1977). Improving the social status of mainstreamed retarded children. *Journal of Educational Psychology, 69,* 605–611.

Bullock, J. (1988). Encouraging the development of social competence in young children. *Early Child Development and Care, 37,* 47–54.

Elliott, S., and Gresham, F. (1991). *Social skills intervention guide: Practical strategies for social skill training*. Circle Pines, MN: American Guidance Service.

Gajewski, N., and Mayo, P. (1989a). *SSS: Social skill strategies (Book A)*. Eau Claire, WI: Thinking Publications.

Gajewski, N., and Mayo, P. (1989b). *SSS: Social skill strategies (Book B)*. Eau Claire, WI: Thinking Publications.

Gresham, F. (1981). Social skills training with handicapped children: A review. *Review of Education Research, 51,* 139–176.

Gresham, F. (1984). Social skills and self-efficacy for exceptional children. *Exceptional Children, 51*(2), 253–259.

Goldstein, A., Sprafkin, R., Gershaw, N., and Klein, P. (1980). *Skillstreaming the adolescent: A structured learning approach to teaching prosocial skills*. Champaign, IL: Research Press.

Hazel, J., Schumaker, J., Sherman, J., and Sheldon-Wildgen, J. (1980). *Asset: A social skills program for adolescents*. Champaign, IL: Research Press.

Madden, N., and Slavin, R. (1983). Mainstreaming students with mild handicaps: Academic and social outcomes. *Journal of Education Research, 53,* 519–569.

McGinnis, E., Goldstein, A., Sprafkin, R., and Gershaw, N. (1984). *Skillstreaming the elementary school child: A guide for teaching prosocial skills.* Champaign, IL: Research Press.

Nippold, M. (Ed.). (1994). Pragmatics and social skills in school-age children and adolescents. *Topics in Language Disorders, 14*(3).

Schumaker, J., and Hazel, J. (1984a). Social skill assessment and training for the learning disabled: Who's on first and what's on second? (Part One). *Journal of Learning Disabilities, 17*(7), 422–429.

Schumaker, J., and Hazel, J. (1984b). Social skill assessment and training for the learning disabled: Who's on first and what's on second? (Part Two). *Journal of Learning Disabilities, 17*(8), 492–499.

Stephans, T. (1978). *Social skills in the classroom.* Columbus, OH: Cedars Press.

Strain, P., Odom, S., and McConnell. S. (1984). Promoting social reciprocity of exceptional children: Identification of target behavior selection and intervention. *Remedial and Special Education, 5,* 21–28.

**Beth:** What am I supposed to do? How am I supposed to get John to at least look at other people?

**Ms. Green:** I don't know, honey. Maybe if John knows that you will be his friend, he will be able to gain more confidence.

[*That evening John and Beth go to a movie and to a restaurant.*]

**Beth:** What did you think about the movie?

**John:** It was OK. I've seen better.

**Beth:** [*In a gentle voice*] John, I really like being with you. We've known each other for a long time, but I don't understand why you never look at me. Is there something wrong with me? I feel uncomfortable being around you.

**John:** [*Looking up briefly*] I'm sorry I make you feel that way. It's just that I never know what people think about me. I guess I'm afraid to look at them.

[*The scene ends as John and Beth continue their conversation in the restaurant.*]

**Definition of Skill:**    Behaving or acting politely

**Skill Activities/ Discussions:**

1. Ask students to provide personal experiences of times when they have been around others who have used manners or who have not used manners. Have the students discuss how they felt.

2. Make a list with the students of as many manners as they can think of during a specified period of time. Order the list from most important to least important.

3. Discuss how manners may vary in different situations and with different people.

**Situations:**

### Home
A concert with your favorite group is playing in your city. You want to go but you don't have the money. Use manners when you ask you parents for some extra money.

### School
It's between classes at school. The halls are crowded. Accidentally, you bump into another student, knocking her books over. Use manners in this situation.

### Community
You are in a hurry. Your mom sent you to the store to buy ice cream. The man in front of you in the checkout line has a basket full of groceries. Use manners when you ask him if you could go in front of him to check out first.

## Script **A** Manners

| | |
|---|---|
| **Number of Characters:** | 4 |
| **Character Description:** | Mom—Parent of Josh, Renee, and Andy |
| | Josh—A fourteen-year-old boy |
| | Renee—A twelve-year-old girl |
| | Andy—A seven-year-old boy |
| **Scene Description:** | This scene takes place at home. The other parent, who is not in the script, has invited his boss over for dinner. |

**Mom:** Hurry up, Josh! They will be here any minute.

**Josh:** I'm coming, Mom! Gee, I don't know what all of the fuss is about. You'd think the President of the U.S. and the Queen of England were coming for supper.

**Mom:** Renee, how are you doing? Are you dressed yet?

**Renee:** I'm coming. I'll be dressed soon.

**Mom:** Andy, let's see your fingernails. Did you get them clean?

**Andy:** Mom, what's so special? You're making everyone miserable. I even had to take a bath!

*[All three children stand in front of their mother.]*

**Mom:** OK, you three. Let's go over the manners again. Andy, when do we begin to eat?

**Andy:** When everyone has the food.

**Mom:** Renee, what do you say when you're introduced to Mr. Simon?

**Renee:** How about if I say, "Hi ya, buddy?"

*[The children start laughing and get an impatient look from their mom.]*

---

**Renee:** Oh, all right, Mom. I'm going to say, "Hi, Mr. Simon. It's nice to meet you."

**Mom:** One last question, Josh. When do you get up after we have finished eating?

**Josh:** After everyone is finished.

**Andy:** Do we really have to sit that long at the table?

**Mom:** Yes, we do. I know this dinner is going to demand a lot from you, but it's important to your dad that everything goes well.

*[Mom pauses to listen to the doorbell.]*

**Mom:** There they are now. Let's get ready.

**Number of Characters:** 6

**Character Description:** Helen—Mother of Larissa, Lorna, and Stuart

Ben—Father of Larissa, Lorna, and Stuart

Stuart—A fourteen-year-old boy

George—Uncle of Larissa, Lorna, and Stuart

Larissa—A sixteen-year-old girl

Lorna—A twelve-year-old girl

**Scene Description:** Ben has been talking to George on the phone. The scene begins when Ben says good-bye and hangs up.

**Ben:** Helen, guess who was just on the phone?

**Helen:** I don't know. Who?

**Ben:** Uncle George, and I invited him for dinner in fifteen minutes.

**Helen:** *[Frowning]* Oh Ben. Is George really coming for dinner? I can't stand to watch him eat. George is a very kind and generous person, but what a pig!

*[A short while later the doorbell rings. Ben goes to answer the door, while Helen puts food on the table. George comes in and rushes straight to the table.]*

**George:** It's sure nice to see you all again. Hey, Stuart, pass me some of that meat. Looks like I came on the right night. There ain't nothing better than a roast. Ben, what are you taking so long with the butter for? Get it over here. Time's wasting!

**Larissa:** George, would you like a roll?

**George:** Sure, Larissa. Pick out a nice one for me and throw it here!

**Lorna:** Mom, would you please pass the gravy? I . . .

*[Uncle George interrupts.]*

**George:** Hey Helen! Since that gravy is going down to the other end of the table, pass it my way first.

**Stuart:** George, about how long are you going to be in town?

**George:** About a week. I bought presents for all of you. *[Burping loudly]* Nothin' like a good burp to make room for dessert.

| **Skill** | 3 | **Volume** |

**Definition of Skill:** Speaking in a voice that can be heard easily, neither too loudly, nor too softly

**Skill Activities/ Discussions:**

1. Ask for two student volunteers. Have one talk to the class in a soft voice. Have the second student talk in a loud voice. Conduct a class discussion about the demonstration.

2. Brainstorm a list of times when speaking in a loud voice is appropriate; when speaking in a soft voice is appropriate.

3. Ask students to practice appropriate ways of asking others to speak louder or softer.

**Situations:**

**Home**

Your very shy sister never talks above a whisper. Demonstrate how you would tell her that using the correct volume is important.

**School**

It's the first day of school. Your teacher wants you to say five facts about yourself aloud to the other students. There are 30 students in your class. Demonstrate the use of an appropriate volume as you give five facts.

**Community**

You have looked all over the store for a new soft drink. Ask a clerk where it is located, using an appropriate volume when asking.

## Script A — Volume

| | |
|---|---|
| **Number of Characters:** | 4 |
| **Character Description:** | Mr. Jonas—A sales trainer |
| | Ms. Gray—A student salesperson |
| | Mr. Cran—A student salesperson |
| | Ms. Bell—A student salesperson |
| **Scene Description:** | The scene takes place in an office. A group of students are being trained for their summer job of door-to-door magazine sales. |

**Mr. Jonas:** During this session, we are going to talk about some communication techniques that will help you manage the volume of your voice.

**Ms. Gray:** What does volume have to do with selling magazines?

**Mr. Jonas:** That's a good question. For example, what would happen if one of our salespersons went up to a customer and talked like this *[whispering]*, "Hello, I'm from Thrifty Magazines . . ?"

**Mr. Cran:** Could you speak up, please? We can't hear you.

**Mr. Jonas:** Exactly. How can we expect to sell magazines if we can't be heard? *[Talking loudly]* And what about the person who talks like this?

**Ms. Gray:** He isn't going to sell many magazines either.

**Mr. Jonas:** Usually, the volume rule is to speak to customers in a normal tone of voice. Use the same volume that you use with your friends and family.

**Ms. Bell:** Mr. Jonas, your rule is rather obvious. I don't think that any of us would shout or whisper to a customer. How do we know if we have the right volume?

---

**Mr. Jonas:**  As with many other communication skills, you need to take cues from the situation. Are both you and the customer comfortable? Does the customer keep asking you to speak up? Is the customer trying to back away because your sales pitch is too loud? All of these cues will help you to evaluate the situation.

**Mr. Cran:**  I understand those cues. What about the times when we have to speak louder or softer?

**Mr. Jonas:**  Can you give me an example of those times?

**Ms. Gray:**  How about when you are speaking to an older person?

**Mr. Jonas:**  You have brought up a good point. Don't assume you need to change your volume just because a customer is older or has a hearing impairment. By doing so, you will be putting these people down. Don't make that mistake. Just watch for the cues.

| | |
|---|---|
| **Number of Characters:** | 5 |
| **Character Description:** | Jessie—A waitress |
| | Malcolm—A friend |
| | David—A friend |
| | Karina—A friend |
| | Jan—A friend |
| **Scene Description:** | A group of people have just returned from seeing a thrilling suspense movie. They are sitting in a restaurant, talking very excitedly about the movie. |

**Malcolm:** *[Laughing]* Yeah, I know why you jumped up during that murder scene and went for popcorn. You were scared!

**David:** I wasn't scared, just hungry! Those thriller movies give me an appetite!

**Malcolm:** *[Loudly]* I don't know about the rest of you, but if I could have gotten up during that one scene, I would have! I was too scared to move!

**Karina:** *[Laughing]* That's right! I saw you peeking through your fingers!

**Malcolm:** *[Loudly]* Poking fun at me, huh? What about the time you got so excited you stood up and started shouting at the movie? How embarrassing!

*[Jessie, the waitress, walks up to their table.]*

**Jessie:** I'll be right with you. Could you please quiet down? It sounds like you had a really good time, but some of our customers don't want to hear about it.

**Malcolm:** Yeah, sure.

**David:** *[Whispering]* What was your favorite part in the movie?

**Jan:** What did you say? I know the waitress said to tone down the volume, but I don't think we have to whisper.

**David:** *[In a regular tone of voice]* I said, "What was your favorite part of the movie?"

**Jessie:** *[Interrupting]* Can I take your order?

## Skill 4 — Choosing the Right Time and Place

**Definition of Skill:** Choosing the best time and place to talk about a certain topic

**Skill Activities/ Discussions:**

1. Present three or four examples in which the best time and place were not used to make a request or to give information. Have the students identify the inappropriate use of the skill. Have them suggest a better time and place for each example given.

2. Present students with two or three requests they might want to make (e.g., receiving more allowance, wanting to turn a paper in late). Have the students suggest appropriate times and places to make each request.

3. Develop a handout in which the students match situations to the appropriate times and places.

**Situations:**

**Home**
You want to ask your parents for an increase in your allowance. Tell your audience what the right time and place might be when you role play this situation.

**School**
You want to talk to your teacher about doing some extra credit work. Tell your audience what the right time and place might be when you role play this situation.

**Community**
You want to ask the manager of a local fast-food restaurant for an application to apply for a job. Tell your audience what the right time and place might be when you role play this situation.

| | |
|---|---|
| **Number of Characters:** | 4 |
| **Character Description:** | Willie—A teenager |
| | Mrs. Madsen—Willie's mother |
| | Ronaldo—Willie's friend |
| | Mrs. Manos—Ronaldo's mother |
| **Scene Description:** | Ronaldo has invited Willie to spend the weekend camping with his family. Willie needs to ask permission to go. Willie and Ronaldo rush into Willie's house. Mrs. Madsen is on the phone. |

**Willie:** *[Excitedly]* Hi, Mom! Oops! Sorry. *[Sees Mom on phone.] [Willie says to Ronaldo.]* My mom has been really busy. She's trying to set up a new business.

*[The boys wait until Mrs. Madsen finishes her call.]*

**Willie:** Mom, is this a good time to talk to you? What I mean is, are you busy?

**Mrs. Madsen:** No, Willie. I can see you are excited. What's up?

**Willie:** Ronaldo just asked me to go camping next weekend.

**Ronaldo:** That's right, Mrs. Madsen. My family and I are going camping in the northern part of the state, and we thought Willie might like to come along.

**Willie:** We'll be leaving on Friday around noon, and we should be home early on Sunday.

**Ronaldo:** My mother is going to call you and explain the details.

*[The phone rings.]*

**Mrs. Manos:** Hello, Mrs. Madsen! I suppose the boys have already told you about our camping trip. We would enjoy having Willie come along.

**Mrs. Madsen:** It sounds like fun! I know he would have a good time. Thanks for inviting him.

---

*[Mrs. Madsen and Mrs. Manos talk for awhile longer.*
*Mrs. Madsen hangs up the phone and turns to Willie.]*

**Mrs. Madsen:** I guess it's all set.

**Willie:** That's great! Come on, Ronaldo. Let's go get out my camping gear.

**Ronaldo:** OK.

**Mrs. Madsen:** By the way boys, thanks for being so patient while I was on the phone. Willie, you've had to do a lot of waiting lately.

**Willie:** That's OK, Mom. I know how busy you've been. I was going to ask you at dinner, but then I remembered we were going to have company.

**Mrs. Madsen:** That's right, Willie. You picked the best time and place to ask me about the camping trip. Dinner probably would have been hectic for all of us.

*[The boys leave to look for camping gear.*
*Mrs. Madsen makes another call.]*

| | |
|---|---|
| **Number of Characters:** | 3 |
| **Character Description:** | Reny—A clerk |
| | Mrs. Jakes—The boss |
| | Mrs. Allen—A customer |
| **Scene Description:** | Reny works as a salesclerk in a local store. He wants to ask his boss, Mrs. Jakes, for the day off. The scene begins with Mrs. Jakes waiting on Mrs. Allen. |

**Mrs. Jakes:** This hair dryer is the best that we carry and it's on sale, too!

**Mrs. Allen:** Well, I . . .

**Reny:** *[Interrupting]* Mrs. Jakes, I need to talk to you about something.

**Mrs. Jakes:** Excuse me, Mrs. Allen. I'll be right back.

*[Mrs. Jakes and Reny step aside.]*

**Mrs. Jakes:** I sure hope what you have to say is important.

**Reny:** It's important to me!

**Mrs. Allen:** *[Looking at Mrs. Jakes and Reny]* Excuse me, I have to go soon. Can we finish talking about this hair dryer?

**Mrs. Jakes:** I'll be right with you.

**Reny:** Mrs. Jakes, I was wondering if I can have next Saturday off. You see, I . . .

**Mrs. Jakes:** *[Angrily]* You interrupted me for that! You should ask me that when I'm in the office and not busy with a customer.

*[Mrs. Allen decides she can't wait any longer and walks off.]*

**Mrs. Jakes:** Look at that! Because you picked the wrong time and place to talk to me, we lost a customer!

**Reny:** I'm sorry, Mrs. Jakes.

## Skill 5 — Tone of Voice

**Definition of Skill:**  Showing feelings through voice quality

**Skill Activities/ Discussions:**

1. Pass out cards to students with one "feeling" word written on each card. Choose one student. Have the student sit facing away from each of the other students. Direct the student to display the feeling written on the card. Instruct the rest of the class to try to guess the correct feeling based on the tone of voice used.

2. Discuss these terms: *enthusiasm, showing interest,* and *monotone.* What other terms can be used to describe tone of voice? Have students discuss and illustrate these tones of voice.

3. Have students explain why enthusiasm and interest are important when communicating.

**Situations:**

**Home**
Your parents are angry because you came home an hour late. Use the correct tone of voice as you explain why you were late.

**School**
You have to persuade your class to buy Orange-O, a new kind of soda pop. Use the correct tone of voice as you try to convince them to buy the soda pop.

**Community**
You are a lifeguard at a swimming pool. An eight-year-old boy keeps running on the deck of the pool. Talk to him, using the correct tone of voice. Explain to him why he cannot run by the pool.

| | |
|---|---|
| **Number of Characters:** | 3 |
| **Character Description:** | Greg—A waiter |
| | Mr. Tabs—A customer |
| | Mrs. Tabs—A customer |
| **Scene Description:** | The scene takes place in a restaurant. Greg is helping two customers. His enthusiastic tone of voice pays off. |

**Greg:** *[Enthusiastically]* Good Afternoon! May I help you?

**Mr. Tabs:** Yes, we've been told you have excellent desserts. We would like to try some.

**Greg:** I'll be glad to help you. Right now, we have fifteen different desserts, not counting our ice creams. All of our desserts are made fresh daily. Would you like to see a dessert menu?

**Mrs. Tabs:** Could you suggest something?

**Greg:** Our banana cream pie is delicious. It's very rich. We also have hot apple cobbler, which is great with vanilla ice cream.

**Mrs. Tabs:** The apple cobbler sounds great to me!

**Mr. Tabs:** I'm going to try the pie.

**Greg:** Would you like anything to drink?

**Mrs. Tabs:** Could I have a diet lemon-lime, please?

**Mr. Tabs:** I'd just like water, please.

**Greg:** Thank you for your order. I'll be right back.

**Mr. Tabs:** He sure is a good waiter. He has such a pleasant tone of voice.

**Mrs. Tabs:** He sure does! I'll bet he earns good tips.

| Number of Characters: | 4 |
| --- | --- |
| Character Description: | Kelly—A teenager |
| | Mr. Wylie—Kelly's father |
| | Mrs. Wylie—Kelly's mother |
| | Jeff—Kelly's older brother |
| Scene Description: | Kelly wants to go to a Groosome Twosome concert, but runs into a problem. |

**Kelly:** *[Excitedly]* Hey, Mom! Dad! Guess who's going to be in concert here next month?

**Mrs. Wylie:** I can't guess. Who?

**Kelly:** Groosome Twosome!

**Mr. Wylie:** I thought the city council refused to give them a permit.

**Kelly:** I don't know about that, Dad. But here's the ticket advertisement.

**Mr. Wylie:** My gosh! Fifteen dollars to see those nuts?

**Kelly:** Dad, I really want to go! I've got $15. Can I go?

**Mrs. Wylie:** You want to waste your money on that concert?

**Kelly:** But it isn't a waste! I like Groosome Twosome.

**Mr. Wylie:** Whether you like them or not, you can't go!

**Kelly:** But, Dad, you're not being fair! *[Raising his voice]* I do all those chores around here for you and now you won't let me do anything I want. You just want me to be your slave!

**Mr. Wylie:** Don't shout at me! You can't go and that's final!

**Kelly:** *[Yelling]* It doesn't matter what I want, does it? It's always got to be your way! I'm tired of it!

| | |
|---|---|
| **Mrs. Wylie:** | You had better change that tone of voice quickly! |
| **Jeff:** | Hey, what's all the yelling about? |
| **Mr. Wylie:** | We told Kelly he couldn't go to a Groosome Twosome concert and he's mad. |

*[Jeff takes Kelly into another room.]*

| | |
|---|---|
| **Jeff:** | Hey, kid! You know that yelling at Mom and Dad never gets you anywhere except sent to your room. |
| **Kelly:** | I know. They get me so mad! Everything is fine as long as I do what they want. I'm tired of it! |
| **Jeff:** | Well, shouting at them certainly isn't going to get you to the concert. |

## Skill 6 — Getting to the Point

**Definition of Skill:** Talking about the main topic of the conversation right away

**Skill Activities/ Discussions:**

1. Have students think of reasons why people beat around the bush (for example, when they think the answer will be no, when they are embarrassed, etc.).

2. Discuss how it makes a listener feel when a speaker beats around the bush.

3. Discuss the difference between *beating around the bush* and *procrastination*.

**Situations:**

**Home**
You were given detention at school. Demonstrate how you would tell your parents, getting straight to the point.

**School**
Your teacher is working at her desk. Demonstrate how you would ask for an extension on your homework assignment.

**Community**
You checked out a book from the public library and lost it. Demonstrate how you would tell the librarian. Make sure to get to the point.

| | |
|---|---|
| **Number of Characters:** | 5 |
| **Character Description:** | Kristin Tyson—A teenager |
| | Mr. Tyson—Kristin's father |
| | Sue—A friend |
| | Mr. Olson—The assistant manager |
| | Ms. Brown—The manager |
| **Scene Description:** | Sue is at Kristin's house and they are talking about the camping trip they have been planning all summer. When the scene begins, Kristin finds out she has a problem. |

**Sue:** Oh, yeah! Don't forget to bring your swimming suit and some shoes for hiking. They have some great trails.

**Kristin:** Hiking and swimming? Boy, this camping trip is going to be great! I'm really glad your folks are letting me come along.

**Sue:** I almost forgot to tell you! We'll pick you up Thursday afternoon around 3:00. That way we'll get to the campground before dark.

**Kristin:** Did you say Thursday? I thought we weren't going until Saturday.

**Sue:** No way. We always leave on Thursday. That way we have all day Friday and Saturday and half the day on Sunday. Why? What's the problem?

**Kristin:** Oh, man, I don't believe this. I'm supposed to work Thursday night.

**Mr. Tyson:** Hello, you two! What are you up to?

**Kristin:** Hi, Dad. You know the camping trip Sue is taking me on? Well, I just found out we're supposed to leave Thursday at 3:00 and I have to work.

**Mr. Tyson:** Any chance you can get your schedule changed?

**Kristin:** I think I'll go down there now and ask.

*[Kristin and Sue ride their bikes to where Kristin works.*
*Kristin walks up to the assistant manager.]*

**Kristin:** Hello, Mr. Olson.

**Mr. Olson:** Hello, Kristin. I didn't see you on the schedule today. What are you doing here?

**Kristin:** I have a problem with my schedule. Is Ms. Brown here?

**Mr. Olson:** Yes, but I'll tell you, she is really busy. I don't know if you'll have any luck.

**Kristin:** Well, I better try.

*[Kristin knocks on Ms. Brown's office door.]*

**Ms. Brown:** Come in.

**Kristin:** Hello, Ms. Brown. I know you're busy, but I wonder if I could talk to you for just a minute? Is there any way to change my schedule so I can have Thursday off?

**Ms. Brown:** Check with Bruce. I heard he is looking for someone to switch hours with. He wants next weekend off.

**Kristin:** Thank you. I'll do that.

**Ms. Brown:** Thank you for coming right to the point. I'm really behind today.

**Kristin:** I better let you get back to work. Thank you. I'll check with Bruce. Good-bye.

**Ms. Brown:** Good-bye.

| | |
|---|---|
| **Number of Characters:** | 4 |
| **Character Description:** | Brice—A student |
| | Janell—A friend |
| | Jill—A friend |
| | Steve—A friend |
| **Scene Description:** | Brice wants to go with Janell to the school dance, but is nervous about asking for the date. Jill and Steve, who already have dates, are sitting with Brice at lunch. |

**Jill:** Hey, did you two hear that the student council is going to hire a live band for the dance Friday night?

**Steve:** I did! I can't wait! That dance is going to be excellent. I just wish tomorrow was Friday.

**Jill:** Me, too! Brice, did you ask Janell to go with you yet?

**Brice:** No, not yet.

**Jill:** What's taking you so long? You better ask soon. It's already Wednesday. The dance is in two days.

**Steve:** If you get a date, Brice, then the six of us could go together. We'd have a blast!

**Brice:** You're right. It would be great. Hey, there's Janell sitting over by the window.

**Steve:** Come on, Brice. Go for it! Go ask her now!

*[Brice picks up his lunch tray and walks over to Janell.]*

**Brice:** Hi, Janell. Can I eat lunch with you? I have something I want to ask you.

**Janell:** Sure, have a seat. What's up?

---

**Brice:** Did you hear they are going to have a live band at the dance Friday night?

**Janell:** Yes, I did. They are called the Chain Reaction.

**Brice:** It sure would be fun to hear them play, wouldn't it?

**Janell:** Yeah, it would!

**Brice:** I guess the dance goes from 7:00–10:00.

*[Brice keeps talking to Janell, but never gets to the point of asking her to go with him.]*

**Janell:** The bell is going to ring soon. Didn't you say you had something to ask me?

**Brice:** Yes, I did. Well, a . . . I was wondering if . . . I wanted to know . . .

*[The bell rings and they head off to class. After school, Jill and Steve meet Brice at his locker.]*

**Jill:** Well, what did Janell say?

**Brice:** I didn't exactly ask yet.

**Steve:** What do you mean you didn't ask? You two talked for 15 minutes.

**Brice:** I guess I didn't get a chance.

**Steve:** Look, next time you see Janell, you'd better get straight to the point and ask before someone else does.

**Jill:** No kidding. If you keep beating around the bush, it will be too late.

## Skill 7 — Staying on Topic

**Definition of Skill:** Maintaining a topic of conversation and using appropriate transitional topic shifts

**Skill Activities/ Discussions:**

1. Discuss how a listener may feel when the speaker switches topics without warning.

2. Have the students brainstorm and make a list of several topics that they would like to talk about. Use those topics for a game activity. Game ideas:
   a. Let each student choose a topic and make five different comments about that topic in thirty seconds or less. Time the responses.
   b. Split the group into two teams. Instruct team #1 to make five different comments (the team can purposely make all their comments about just one topic, or they can make them about two, three, four, or five different topics). Instruct team #2 to listen to the comments only once and then guess the number of topics.

3. Discuss what could happen if all of the people in a conversation have a different topic they wish to maintain at the same time. Then have students think of times when they wanted the topic of conversation to change, but the speaker kept talking on and on. Help students to distinguish when a topic of conversation is maintained too long.

**Situations:**

**Home**
You are feeling like you have too much homework and too many house chores. Talk with your mom or dad about your house chores, and make sure all of your comments deal with that topic.

**School**
It is the first day of school, and the teacher has asked you to make some comments about yourself. Tell the teacher a few things about yourself.

**Community**
You are a tour guide. Choose one place in your community and make comments pertaining to that topic.

| | |
|---|---|
| **Number of Characters:** | 4 |
| **Character Description:** | Mr. Welsh—The classroom teacher |
| | Craig—A student |
| | Tracy—A student |
| | Yolanda—A student |
| **Scene Description:** | It is the first day of class. Mr. Welsh, the history teacher, is describing the classroom rules to the students. |

**Mr. Welsh:** The next rule deals with class participation. I really want to hear your ideas and thoughts, so you can expect several class discussions. However, it's very important that all your comments deal with the topic we happen to be discussing at the time.

*[Mr. Welsh sees Tracy's hand up and calls on her.]*

**Tracy:** You mean we can't switch topics?

**Mr. Welsh:** That is exactly right.

**Craig:** What does that mean?

**Mr. Welsh:** That's a good question. Who can explain what switching topics means?

**Yolanda:** Well, if we are all talking about World War II, and someone asks what they are serving for hot lunch, that would be switching topics.

**Mr. Welsh:** Good example! Tracy, I see your hand up.

**Tracy:** We used to do that purposely in science last year. It was really easy to get Mr. Nelson off topic. Then at the end of class, he would have to postpone the homework assignment another day.

*[The students in class start laughing.]*

**Mr. Welsh:** That is exactly why I have included that rule. If we consistently get off topic, what kind of progress would we make?

**Yolanda:** Not much, but at least we wouldn't get as much homework.

**Mr. Welsh:** Would you rather get homework and have to figure out how to do it on your own at home? Or would you like to have time to discuss it thoroughly in class so you know exactly what to do?

**Craig:** OK! We get the message. No switching topics.

**Mr. Welsh:** Great! Now speaking of switching topics, I'd like to do that right now. Let's talk about how you will be graded this year.

## Script **B** Staying on Topic

| | |
|---|---|
| **Number of Characters:** | 3 |
| **Character Description:** | Kristi—A teenager |
| | Mark—A teenager |
| | Lynn—A teenager |
| **Scene Description:** | Mark and Lynn are talking at Mark's locker before school starts. |

**Mark:** So, did you and your cousin see that movie Friday night? I know you said you were thinking about going.

**Lynn:** Yeah, we went to the early show at the Marc Theater.

**Mark:** So, how did you like it?

**Lynn:** It was excellent. You've got to see it.

**Mark:** What was it about and who was in it?

*[Lynn notices Kristi walking toward them.]*

**Lynn:** Hi, Kristi. How's it going?

**Kristi:** Hi, Lynn. Hi, Mark.

**Mark:** Lynn was just telling me about a movie she saw Friday night.

**Kristi:** Oh, yeah? Which movie? By the way, did I tell you I had to baby-sit all weekend?

**Lynn:** All weekend? How many kids did you baby-sit for?

**Kristi:** Right before I went to baby-sit, my dad took me to get a new puppy. It's only six weeks old!

**Mark:** Boy, are you lucky! What kind is it?

**Kristi:** Well, let me think . . . that movie was?

**Lynn:** It was called "Fantasy." Have you seen it? It was great!

**Kristi:** Are you two going to the basketball game this week?

**Mark:** I was thinking about it.

**Kristi:** Did you hear that Steve has to get braces? Oh, wow! Class starts in two minutes! I better get going. I'll see ya later. Bye.

*[Kristi walks down the hall to class.]*

**Lynn:** That conversation sure was confusing.

**Mark:** No kidding! Kristi kept switching topics. She always does that and it bugs me. We never did find out who she baby-sat for or what kind of dog she's gotten. And I didn't get to hear about the movie either. Maybe you can tell me about it during lunch.

**Lynn:** Sounds good. I'll see you then.

**Mark:** Bye.

## Skill 8 — Listening

**Definition of Skill:** Giving full attention to a speaker in order to understand the meaning of the spoken message

**Skill Activities/ Discussions:**

1. Discuss what happens in a conversation when everyone is talking and no one is listening.

2. Discuss how a speaker can tell if a person is listening or not.

3. Write the following sentence where everyone can read it.

   A listener should _____ because _____.

   Have students generate ideas to complete the sentence.

   *Example:* A listener should stop what he or she is doing and face the speaker because then the speaker knows that the listener is paying attention.

4. Brainstorm a list of specific things that can be done to prepare for good listening in class (e.g., sit up straight, don't doodle, focus attention).

**Situations:**

**Home**
Your younger brother comes to you and says he wants to talk to you about a problem he's having with a friend. Demonstrate what you could do when he talks to you, where you should look, and what you could say when he is finished.

**School**
You are talking to your friends. Show what you could do when the announcements start coming over the intercom.

**Community**
You are at a movie. The people sitting behind you are talking so loudly that you are having trouble listening. Demonstrate what you could say to the people to let them know they are distracting you.

**Number of Characteristics:** 3

**Character Description:** Kurt—A teenager

Michelle—Kurt's friend

Sam—Kurt's friend

**Scene Description:** Kurt is planning to finish a math assignment that is due next hour during study hall. He is working on the assignment when Michelle comes up to talk.

**Kurt:** Hi, Michelle!

**Michelle:** *[Looking very depressed]* Hi, Kurt.

**Kurt:** What's wrong, Michelle? You don't look very happy.

**Michelle:** I had a rotten morning. I could sure use someone to talk to. Do you have a minute?

> *[Kurt thinks about trying to do the math assignment and talking to Michelle at the same time, but reconsiders. He can tell Michelle really needs someone to listen.]*

**Kurt:** *[Putting down his pencil]* I've got to get this math done during study hall, but it won't take the whole period. Tell me, what happened?

**Michelle:** My parents grounded me this morning, so now I can't go to the game Friday night.

**Kurt:** Why did you get grounded?

> *[Kurt listens carefully as Michelle tells him what happened.]*

**Michelle:** Well, thanks for listening. I'd better let you get to your homework.

**Kurt:** Sure thing! Hang in there. Tell you what, I'll call your place right after I get home Friday night and tell you all about the game.

*[Kurt notices that there is only 20 minutes left in study hall. He thinks there may be just enough time to finish his math, and gets right to work. Just then Kurt's friend, Sam, walks up.]*

**Sam:** Hi, Kurt!

**Kurt:** How's it going, Sam?

**Sam:** Not bad. We had the best time camping last weekend. I've got to tell you about it.

*[Kurt thinks about the math and the zero he'll get if it isn't done.]*

**Kurt:** I'd really like to hear about it, but I have a problem.

**Sam:** What's that?

**Kurt:** I don't think I would be a very good listener. I have to get this math done in the next 15 minutes.

**Sam:** That's no problem! How about if I call you after school? We can talk then.

**Kurt:** Thanks. I'm glad you had a good time camping.

**Sam:** I'll call tonight. See you.

**Kurt:** Bye.

| | |
|---|---|
| **Number of Characters:** | 3 |
| **Character Description:** | Beth—A teenager |
| | Joe—Beth's brother |
| | Mom—Beth and Joe's mom |
| **Scene Description:** | Beth was in a track meet after school and did really well. She is very excited to get home and tell her family about it. |

**Beth:** *[Walking in the door]* Hi, anybody home?

> *[Beth walks into the family room and finds Joe laying on the floor, singing along with the music on the stereo.]*

**Beth:** Hi, Joe.

**Joe:** Hi.

**Beth:** We had our track meet against Jefferson after school today.

**Joe:** *[Still concentrating on the music]* Oh, yeah?

**Beth:** Yeah, we beat them by 3 points. It was great! I was in the long jump and the 400 meter.

> *[Joe starts snapping his fingers to the music and begins mouthing the words. Beth can tell he isn't interested in hearing about the track meet. She goes to tell her mom about the meet and finds her in the kitchen, repairing a lamp.]*

**Beth:** Hi, Mom.

**Mom:** Oh, hi, Beth. How was school?

**Beth:** OK. We had our track meet after school and I did pretty good in both my events.

*[Beth's mom continues working on the*
*lamp instead of looking at Beth.]*

**Mom:** Oh, yeah?

**Beth:** I took second in the 400 meter and beat my own record by 2 seconds. The coach says he may move me up to varsity for the next meet.

*[Beth's mom starts digging in the toolbox for electrical tape.]*

**Mom:** That's nice! What event did you say that was?

**Beth:** Oh, it doesn't matter. I can tell you're busy with the lamp. I better get started on my homework.

*[Beth walks out of the kitchen, disappointed that*
*no one wanted to hear about her track meet.]*

## Skill 9 — Starting and Ending a Conversation

**Definition of Skill:** Beginning a conversation with a greeting and name (e.g., "Hello, Mrs. Conway," or "Hi, Jeff.")

Ending a conversation with a farewell (e.g., "Good-bye, Mrs. Conway. Have a nice day," or "Bye, Jeff. See you tomorrow.")

(Note: In our experiences, adolescents have greater difficulties ending conversations than they do starting conversations. Therefore, special emphasis should be placed on the second half of this social communication skill.)

**Skill Activities/ Discussions:**

1. Discuss the importance of a greeting and introduction when making a phone call.

2. Discuss the idea that when speaking to an adult, or wanting to show respect, generally people should say, "Hello, Mr./Mrs. _____." When speaking to peers or good friends, people can be less formal and say, "Hi," and just a first name.

3. Give examples of greeting and farewell forms in foreign languages.

**Situations:**

**Home**
Your mom or dad is reading the paper. Demonstrate how you would ask if you can spend the night at a friend's house. Remember to open and close the conversation.

**School**
You were asked to run an errand to the school office. Demonstrate how you would ask the secretary in the office if you can have a box of staples for one of your teachers. Remember, you are speaking to an adult.

**Community**
You ordered a sweater through a catalog company. Demonstrate how you would stop at the catalog counter to see if your order is in yet. Remember to open and close the conversation.

| | |
|---|---|
| **Number of Characters:** | 4 |
| **Character Description:** | April Jackson—A teenager |
| | Mr. Jackson—April's dad |
| | Ms. Bowen—The secretary |
| | Mr. Knack—The boss |
| **Scene Description:** | April is just about ready to leave for a job interview. The scene begins with Mr. Jackson giving April some last minute advice. |

**April:** I'd better get going. I want to be on time. How do I look?

**Mr. Jackson:** You look very nice and that's important when you interview.

**April:** I think I remember everything we've talked about. Any last minute advice.

**Mr. Jackson:** Don't forget to start and end the interview smoothly. You want to make a good impression the second you walk through the door and you want to leave on a positive note also.

**April:** I know how to begin the interview, but I don't know about the end.

**Mr. Jackson:** Well, you could say something like, "Good-bye, Mr. Knack. Thank you for the interview. I'm looking forward to hearing from you. I know I can do a good job for you."

**April:** That sounds good! Could you write that down for me?

**Mr. Jackson:** Very funny! You'd better get going. Good luck.

**April:** Thanks, Dad. Bye.

*[April arrives at her interview and checks with the secretary.]*

**April:** Excuse me. Hello, my name is April Jackson. I have an interview with Mr. Knack at 2:00.

**Ms. Bowen:** Yes, Ms. Jackson, Mr. Knack is expecting you. His office is to your right.

**April:** Thank you.

*[April walks over and knocks on Mr. Knack's door.]*

**Mr. Knack:** Come in.

*[April stands up straight and smiles as she enters.]*

**April:** Hello, Mr. Knack. It's a pleasure to meet you. I've been looking forward to this interview.

**Mr. Knack:** You have? Most people are very nervous when it comes to interviews.

**April:** Oh, I'm nervous too. But I'd really like this job and I know you need to interview all the applicants.

**Mr. Knack:** Why don't you have a seat and begin by telling me a little about yourself?

*[April begins to relax during the interview. She remembers to end the conversation just as politely as it was started.]*

| | |
|---|---|
| **Number of Characters:** | 3 |
| **Character Description:** | Juan—A friend |
| | Ronda—A friend |
| | Paul—A friend |
| **Scene Description:** | Juan and Ronda are waiting in line together at the movie theater for the early show. The scene begins when the two of them are talking about Paul. |

**Juan:** This movie must be great! I can't believe how long this line is.

**Ronda:** Maybe we should have gotten here earlier. I hope we get in. Speaking of lines, you wouldn't believe what Paul did to me in the lunch line at school today.

**Juan:** I can just imagine. What was it this time?

**Ronda:** Paul came up from behind me and knocked my sack lunch on the floor. My chips flew all over and all Paul had to say about it was, "Sorry about that. You should hang on tighter next time."

**Juan:** Just once I'd like to see Paul start a conversation like a normal person and say, "Hi, Juan. How's it going?"

**Ronda:** I know what you mean. To make matters worse, Paul walked away when he saw Steve in the lunch line, without so much as a good-bye, and left me picking up my lunch off the floor.

**Juan:** I can't believe it. Paul didn't even say good-bye?

**Ronda:** Are you kidding?

**Juan:** Oh, speaking of the devil, guess who just got here?

**Ronda:** *[Turns around quickly]* Let's just hope Paul doesn't see us.

*[Paul sees Juan and Ronda and is happy to see people he knows at the movie. Paul hopes they invite him to sit with them. Paul decides to surprise them and sneaks around from behind.]*

**Juan:** Do you think Paul saw us?

**Ronda:** No, I don't think so.

*[Just then, Paul hits Juan and Ronda on their backs and says in a loud voice . . .]*

**Paul:** So, I see you two are going to the movie, too. How are you doing?

**Juan:** We *were* doing fine.

**Ronda:** Come on, Juan. I don't think we're going to get in. Let's come back for the late show.

*[Ronda and Juan walk away, leaving Paul behind.]*

**Definition of Skill:**   Standing at a proper distance while talking to people

**Skill Activities/ Discussions:**

1. Before introducing the skill, write the word *proximity* where everyone can see it. To increase the students' interest, have them guess what it means.

2. Have the students make a list of times when they would want to stand close, or an arm's length away, or far away from someone (e.g., close—when you are whispering; arm's length—when you are being introduced; far—when a stranger asks for directions).

3. Discuss how the rules for proximity change for different cultures (e.g., people stand closer together in Italian and Puerto Rican communities).

**Situations:**   **Home**

Your mom or dad has invited a new coworker to dinner. Demonstrate how close you would stand when you are introduced.

**School**

You go back to school about 5:00 because you forgot a book. Demonstrate how close you would stand to the custodian when he or she asks why you are in the building.

**Community**

You and a good friend are walking downtown together. Demonstrate an appropriate and inappropriate distance to walk comfortably.

# Script  A  Proximity

| | |
|---|---|
| **Number of Characters:** | 5 |
| **Character Description:** | Maria—The president of the student council |
| | Sid—The vice-president of the student council |
| | Gordy—The secretary of the student council |
| | Megan—A member of the student council |
| | Ed—A member of the student council |
| **Scene Description:** | The student council is meeting. They have already heard the minutes from the last meeting and the treasurer's report. Next, they will discuss new business. |

**Maria:** Let's go on to new business. The first thing on the agenda is the presentation at the elementary school. The principal at Riverside Elementary asked us if we would give a program to their fourth and fifth graders.

**Megan:** What is the program supposed to be about?

**Maria:** Gordy, why don't you tell us more about the presentation? You were the one who talked to the principal at Riverside?

**Gordy:** Sure. They want us to talk to the kids about dealing with strangers. They want us to talk for about 30 minutes.

**Ed:** I think that sounds like a good idea!

**Sid:** I make a motion that we agree to do it.

**Ed:** I second it.

**Maria:** All those in favor, signify by raising your hand.

*[Everyone on the council raises their hand.]*

**Sid:** When are we giving this talk?

**Gordy:** Next week, so we better start planning today.

---

**Maria:** OK. Let's make a list of what we'd like to say.

**Megan:** We were learning about proximity in our social skills class today. Maybe we should talk to the kids about that.

**Sid:** You and your big words. What's "proimity?"

**Megan:** PROXIMITY! It means how close you stand to someone.

**Ed:** Oh, I get it! We should tell those kids that they shouldn't stand close when a stranger talks to them.

**Gordy:** What if the kids ask *why*?

**Megan:** Then we tell them it's because we don't want the stranger to hurt them. If they are standing too close, it would be easy for the stranger to grab them.

**Ed:** I've heard of missing children. I'll bet that's how it happens to a lot of them.

**Sid:** We don't want them to think they should always stand far away when they are talking to anyone!

**Maria:** You mean like when they are talking to a good friend or their parents, it's OK to stand closer.

**Sid:** Right!

**Megan:** Hey, I've got a good idea! How about if we put on two different role plays for the kids?

**Gordy:** Yeah! In one of the plays, we could show how to increase distance when you talk to a stranger. In the other play, we could show how close to stand with a good friend.

**Ed:** You know how kids are. They probably would have more fun watching plays anyway.

**Maria:** Good ideas! What else should we talk about besides proximity?

*[The student council continues to plan their program.]*

## Script B — Proximity

| | |
|---|---|
| **Number of Characters:** | 3 |
| **Character Description:** | Ian—A teenager |
| | Clair—Ian's friend |
| | Yolanda—Clair's cousin |
| **Scene Description:** | Clair is at the mall shopping with her cousin, Yolanda, who is visiting from a different city. They run into Ian in front of the water fountain. |

**Clair:** Hi, Ian!

**Ian:** Hi, Clair! What are you up to?

**Clair:** Yolanda and I came to get some new CDs. Have you ever met my cousin?

**Ian:** No, I haven't.

**Clair:** Ian, this is Yolanda. Yolanda, this is Ian, a friend from school. Yolanda is from Michigan. She is spending the week with my family.

*[Yolanda walks up and stands really close to Ian.]*

**Yolanda:** It's nice to meet you. What are you shopping for?

*[Ian takes a step or two backwards.]*

**Ian:** Nothing really, I just came to look around. What CDs are you going to get?

*[Yolanda walks closer to Ian again.]*

**Yolanda:** We're not sure. We thought we'd look through everything.

*[Ian backs up again.]*

**Ian:** I better get going. I'll see you later. Bye.

| | |
|---|---|
| **Clair:** | Bye, Ian. |
| **Yolanda:** | I wonder why Ian took off so fast. We barely talked. |
| **Clair:** | It doesn't surprise me at all. |
| **Yolanda:** | What do you mean? |
| **Clair:** | I think Ian left because you were standing too close and it made him nervous. |
| **Yolanda:** | I was just trying to be friendly. |
| **Clair:** | Didn't you see that Ian kept backing away? Can't you take a hint? |
| **Yolanda:** | I guess I must be a jerk. |
| **Clair:** | No, you're not a jerk. Just remember to stand back about an arm's length away, especially when you're meeting someone for the first time. |
| **Yolanda:** | You know, not everyone stands that far apart. |
| **Clair:** | True. People in some other cultures don't. But neither you nor Ian are from cultures where people stand that close. Hey, let's go find some CDs. |

*[Clair changes the topic so Yolanda doesn't feel bad.]*

# Skill 11 — Formal/Informal Language

**Definition of Skill:**
- Using special manners in specific situations or with individuals in respected positions (formal language)

- Using colloquialisms and slang directed toward friends, relatives, or others close to the speaker's age (informal language)

**Skill Activities/ Discussions:**

1. Have students compare the way they would talk with a close friend to the way they would talk with a very important person.

2. Provide the students with a variety of situations in which people are talking. Direct the students to identify the situations as formal or informal.

3. Make a list of formal and informal phrases. Discuss when they are used. Use the following as examples: "It's a pleasure to meet you, ladies and gentlemen," "What's going on?", "What's up?", or "You bet!"

**Situations:**

**Home**
Formal: Your father has invited his boss home for dinner. Greet the boss, using formal language.

Informal: Your parents have given you permission to invite a friend along on a canoe trip. Call your friend on the phone and use informal language when you invite him or her.

**School**
Formal: Your grandfather is visiting your school on Parents' Night. Using formal language, demonstrate how you can help start a conversation between your grandfather and the principal.

Informal: You are eating lunch with a friend at school. Talk about the upcoming dance.

**Community:** Formal: You need to talk with the manager of your city regarding the need for a Teen Center. Demonstrate your discussion, using formal language.

Informal: You meet a family friend downtown. Even though he's not your uncle, you call him uncle anyway. Talk to him about your upcoming camping trip.

| | |
|---|---|
| **Number of Characters:** | 3 |
| **Character Description:** | Jason—A high school student |
| | Mr. Mareno—The managing editor of the local paper |
| | Ms. Ling—The receptionist |
| **Scene Description:** | Jason is applying for the job of student writer for the local newspaper. The scene begins as Jason walks into the reception area. |

**Jason:** Excuse me. My name is Jason Kohl. I believe I am scheduled for an interview with Mr. Mareno at 2:00.

**Ms. Ling:** Jason, Mr. Mareno is expecting you. I'll let him know that you've arrived.

**Jason:** Thank you.

**Mr. Mareno:** *[Coming out of his office]* You must be Jason! I have heard a great deal about your writing. Come into my office.

**Jason:** Thank you, sir.

**Mr. Mareno:** Now, why don't you tell me a little about yourself?

**Jason:** Well, to start with, I was born and raised in this town. I feel that I know it quite well. I enjoy and participate in a variety of sports. I try to maintain good grades in school.

**Mr. Mareno:** Very commendable! I see from your application that you want to be a journalist. Please tell me why you are interested in journalism.

**Jason:** Sir, I've never been good at drawing. But I enjoy painting pictures with words. I try to get as much detail into my writing as a painter puts into his pictures.

**Mr. Mareno:** I have to tell you, Jason, that I am very impressed.

**Jason:** Thank you, sir.

**Mr. Mareno:** I'll discuss my impressions with my coworkers and contact you by Wednesday.

**Jason:** Thank you for this opportunity. I've enjoyed our conversation. It's been a pleasure meeting you. Good-bye.

*[Mr. Mareno walks out of his office behind Jason.*
*After Jason leaves, he turns to Ms. Ling.]*

**Mr. Mareno:** What a nice young man! He certainly knows how to conduct himself in an office. So many young people in our community do not know what to do in more formal situations. Jason certainly does!

*[Mr. Mareno goes back into his office.]*

| | |
|---|---|
| **Number of Characters:** | 5 |
| **Character Description:** | Whitney—A sixteen-year-old |
| | Scott—An eleven-year-old |
| | Mr. Sim—Whitney and Scott's dad |
| | Mrs. Sim—Whitney and Scott's mom |
| | Liam—Whitney's friend |
| **Scene Description:** | Whitney invites Liam, a friend, over for dinner at her house. |

**Whitney:** Mom and Dad, I'd like you to meet Liam.

**Mrs. Sim:** Hello, Liam! It's a pleasure to meet you.

**Liam:** Yeah, that's likewise for me, too!

**Mr. Sim:** I understand that you are out of school. What are you doing with your time?

**Liam:** Right now, I'm not doin' much. I finished with the old book grind last spring, and I've been just sort of hangin' out and relaxin' since then.

**Scott:** Relaxing from school?

**Liam:** Sure, kid! School's work, and I've been takin' sort of a vacation.

**Mrs. Sim:** Well, after your vacation, what do you want to do?

**Liam:** I'm plannin' to take a nice long vacation, so I ain't thought of nothin' to do yet. When I have to think of somethin', I will.

**Whitney:** But you do a lot nice things in your spare time.

**Liam:** Sure, sure. I keep busy. I've been buildin' lots of kites. I like kites. They're a hobby of mine.

*[Everyone eats dinner and continues talking.]*

**Mrs. Sim:** Well, Mr. Sim and I have plans for this evening. We had better go. It's been interesting talking with you.

**Liam:** Like I said before, likewise to meeting you, too. Do you mind if I call you by your first names? After all, I am eighteen and we just had this great spread together. I'm just about like family.

*[Mr. and Mrs. Sim leave.]*

**Liam:** Whitney, your ma and dad are OK, but I don't think they liked me. What did I do wrong?

**Whitney:** Oh, nothing. You know parents. They always act that way.

**Liam:** Well, OK. Thanks for dinner. See you tomorrow.

*[The next day . . .]*

**Mrs. Sim:** That young man you've been seeing is, well, ah . . . different.

**Whitney:** I know, Mom. You're used to guys with more polish, but Liam is really a nice guy.

**Mrs. Sim:** I guess you're the one who wants to go out with him. I just wish that he would use more manners and put some endings on his words. I can't imagine someone graduating from high school and still talking about "buildin' kites."

**Whitney:** Right, Mom, I get the picture.

**Mrs. Sim:** Sorry, Whitney. I'm preaching again. I just don't understand how young people expect to handle more formal social situations when they always act so informally.

## Skill 12 — Making a Good Impression

**Definition of Skill:** Making other people think favorably about you because of your actions, appearance, or personal qualities

**Skill Activities/ Discussions:**

1. Collect a variety of pictures of people from magazines or other sources. Show the pictures to the class. Ask what they think the people in the pictures are like. Also, ask which of the people they would like to meet and why. After the students have answered these questions, introduce the phrase *making a good impression*—based upon how a person looks or acts.

2. Make a list of things people do or say that makes a positive or negative impression.

3. Discuss the reasons why an individual may want to make a good impression.

**Situations:**

**Home**
Your friend introduces you to his parents. Make a good impression during the introduction.

**School**
Your English teacher just seated a new student next to you. Make a good impression on this student by offering to help the student find the way around school.

**Community**
You need to find Grant Street. You stop and ask two police officers for directions. Make a good impression when you ask.

| | |
|---|---|
| **Number of Characters:** | 4 |
| **Character Description:** | Cary—A teenager |
| | Josh—Cary's friend |
| | Mrs. Gram—Cary's mother |
| | Mr. Gram—Cary's father |
| **Scene Description:** | Josh has been invited over to Cary's house for dinner. He is meeting Cary's parents for the first time. |

**Cary:** Mom and Dad, I'd like you to meet Josh. Josh, these are my parents.

**Josh:** How do you do, Mr. and Mrs. Gram? Whatever we are having for dinner smells great!

**Mrs. Gram:** Thank you! I'm making Cary's favorite meal.

**Josh:** May I help?

**Mrs. Gram:** That's very nice of you to offer. If you would like to set the table, I would really appreciate it.

**Josh:** No problem. Maybe Cary can show me where the dishes are kept.

**Cary:** Sure, I'd be glad to!

*[Mr. and Mrs. Gram are in the kitchen, while Josh and Cary are setting the table in the dining room.]*

**Mrs. Gram:** Isn't Josh a nice friend for Cary? I really like the way he offered to help right away.

**Mr. Gram:** I couldn't help noticing the way he's dressed. His clothes aren't fancy, but they're clean and his shirt is tucked in.

*[Everyone sits down to eat.]*

**Mrs. Gram:** Are you new in town, Josh?

**Josh:** We've lived here for about a year.

**Mrs. Gram:** Where did you live before moving here?

**Josh:** Actually, I lived in about six cities. My father is in sales. He gets transferred almost every two years.

**Cary:** It must be hard having to move all of the time.

**Josh:** It's not easy having to make new friends all of the time. But in one way, I'm lucky. I've been able to see lots of places and make lots of friends. Mrs. Gram, your dinner is delicious! May I have some more lasagna, please?

**Mrs. Gram:** Certainly! Help yourself!

**Josh:** Thank you.

*[Later that evening, after Josh has gone home.]*

**Mr. Gram:** Josh sure is a nice person. He definitely made a good impression on us. He was considerate and is well-mannered.

**Mrs. Gram:** He's welcome to come over anytime!

## Script B — Making a Good Impression

| | |
|---|---|
| **Number of Characters:** | 2 |
| **Character Description:** | Juan—A teenager |
| | Mr. Meltz—The manager |
| **Scene Description:** | Juan is interviewing for a pizza delivery job. |

**Mr. Meltz:** Come in, Juan. You were so late, I was thinking about leaving.

**Juan:** I know, Mr. Meltz. I just overslept. You see I stayed up watching the late movie and I just couldn't wake up.

**Mr. Meltz:** I see. Is that why your clothes are wrinkled and your hair isn't combed?

**Juan:** Yeah, I guess so. If I had cleaned up, I would have been even later.

**Mr. Meltz:** Are you usually late for your appointments?

**Juan:** Well, most of the time, I'm on time. I was only tardy to school six times last year.

**Mr. Meltz:** Could you tell me why you want this job?

**Juan:** Just like everybody else, I like money. I could use some extra right now. By the way, what does the job pay?

**Mr. Meltz:** We pay minimum wage to start.

**Juan:** Gee, is there any way I could make more money? I'm trying to save up for roller blades.

**Mr. Meltz:** You may be able to get more on a different job. I suggest you apply elsewhere. To be honest, you didn't make a very good impression. On your next interview, try to get there on time, and wear clean clothes.

**Juan:** I guess I should've stayed in bed. It sure hasn't been my day.

**Mr. Meltz:** Maybe you should think about how you would do it all differently, if you had the chance.

**Juan:** Yeah, OK. Good-bye.

*[Juan leaves Mr. Meltz's office.]*

# Skill 13 Interrupting

**Definition of Skill:** Breaking into a conversation that two or more people are having, to deliver a message or comment

**Skill Activities/ Discussions:**

1. Provide students with several situations in which an interruption is necessary. Have the students explain how they are going to interrupt.

2. Brainstorm a list of times when interrupting is necessary and times when it is not.

3. Have people discuss their feelings when someone they know "barges" (interrupts) into a conversation in an inappropriate way.

**Situations:**

**Home**

Your mother is on the phone. Interrupt your mother to tell her that someone is at the front door waiting to talk to her.

**School**

As you approach Room 214, you notice that Ms. Wildman is giving a lecture. Interrupt her to deliver a message from the office.

**Community**

Two clerks are talking in a store. Interrupt them to ask where the bathing suits are located.

| | |
|---|---|
| **Number of Characters:** | 4 |
| **Character Description:** | Ms. Jones—The receptionist |
| | Mr. Bob Abt—The director of advertising |
| | Ms. Green—The boss |
| | Mr. Oakland—The salesperson |
| **Scene Description:** | Ms. Jones has a summer job working as a receptionist in an office. She needs to interrupt Mr. Abt and Ms. Green, as someone is waiting to see Ms. Green. |

*[A salesperson, Mr. Oakland, enters the reception area.]*

**Ms. Jones:** Hello, may I help you?

**Mr. Oakland:** Yes, my name is Mr. Oakland. I am from Moody Products. I have an appointment to see Ms. Green.

**Ms. Jones:** Please, make yourself comfortable. I'll let Ms. Green know you are here. She's expecting you.

*[Ms. Jones knocks on Ms. Green's door and sees her talking with Mr. Abt.]*

**Ms. Green:** I'm not sure if we should pay that large amount of money to advertise on television.

**Mr. Abt:** I know it's a lot. But the audience will be large too. We should be able to increase our products by 50%.

**Ms. Jones:** Excuse me, I'm sorry to interrupt. Mr. Oakland, from Moody Products, is waiting to see Ms. Green.

**Ms. Green:** Sure. I'll be glad to see him! Show him in. Bob, we can finish our discussion during lunch.

*[Ms. Jones goes back to tell Mr. Oakland to go into Ms. Green's office.]*

**Mr. Abt:** That secretary is really good! She looks so young!

**Ms. Green:** She is. She is only a high school student. She does everything from handling complaints to . . .

**Mr. Abt:** Interrupting two talkative business associates.

**Ms. Green:** *[Smiles]* Right. See you at lunch, Bob, we'll finish our discussion.

*[Bob leaves and Mr. Oakland begins talking with Ms. Green.]*

| | |
|---|---|
| **Number of Characters:** | 3 |
| **Character Description:** | Jeff—A teenager |
| | Lindsey—Jeff's girlfriend |
| | Adam—A teenager |
| **Scene Description:** | Jeff and Lindsey are walking down the street holding hands and talking. Adam "barges" into the conversation. |

**Jeff:** I'm sure glad I got my biology test over with.

**Lindsey:** I bet you feel a whole lot better, now that it's over.

**Jeff:** You bet I do. I've never been so nervous over a test before.

**Lindsey:** What should we do this weekend?

**Jeff:** Sandy and Joe are . . .

*[Adam runs up and pushes between Jeff and Lindsey.]*

**Adam:** Hi, guys! Isn't it great? It's Friday!

**Jeff:** *[In a bored voice]* Hi, Adam.

**Lindsey:** Hi, Adam.

**Adam:** What are you doing this weekend?

**Lindsey:** We were just talking about it, but somebody had to interrupt.

**Adam:** Hey! What's the big deal? I just saw you in front of me. I thought it would be unfriendly if I didn't stop and talk.

**Jeff:** I just want some time to talk to Lindsey alone. I'll call you later.

**Adam:** OK. See you two later. Bye.

**Jeff:** Bye.

*[Adam leaves while Jeff and Lindsey continue talking.]*

# Skill 14 — Planning What to Say

**Definition of Skill:** Thinking ahead of time about what is going to be said in a conversation

**Skill Activities/ Discussions:**

1. Develop a list with the students of occasions when it is necessary to plan a conversation ahead of time.

2. Have students discuss feelings they had when they did not plan ahead, and they went into an important conversation unprepared.

3. Provide students with several situations in which planning ahead is necessary. Have the students describe how they will "think ahead" to organize their conversation.

**Situations:**

**Home**
You accidentally broke one of your mother's favorite plates. How are you going to tell her? Discuss how you are going to plan ahead.

**School**
You want to ask a friend to go with you to the school picnic. What are you going to say? Plan your conversation ahead of time.

**Community**
You have a job interview for a position in a clothing store. What are you going to say? Try to plan ahead.

# Script **A** Planning What to Say

| | |
|---|---|
| **Number of Characters:** | 3 |
| **Character Description:** | Grayson—A teenager |
| | Mandy—A teenager |
| | Alex—A teenager |
| **Scene Description:** | Grayson has an interview for a job. He is discussing the interview with two friends. |

**Grayson:** Did I tell you I have a job interview down at Fuller's Department Store? It sure would be nice if I could get that job. I would get 15% off everything I buy!

**Mandy:** Aren't you nervous?

**Grayson:** I sure am! It wouldn't be so bad if I knew what Ms. Garsky, the store manager, was going to say.

**Alex:** Well, why don't we try to think of what she might ask?

**Grayson:** Hey, that's a good idea!

**Mandy:** Well, you can plan on the usual stuff like your age, and what grade you're in. She is probably going to ask you about your grades.

**Alex:** She might also ask you about how much studying you do each evening.

**Grayson:** Why would she ask that?

**Alex:** Because she may want to know if you'll have time to work.

**Grayson:** I'll bet she will ask me when I am available to work. She'll probably also want to know if I have a work permit.

**Mandy:** I've always heard that it's not only important how you answer the questions the interviewer asks, but that you ask some questions, too!

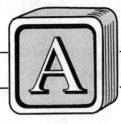

**Grayson:** I've been thinking about that, too. I would want to ask what type of work I'll be doing and maybe how much money I'll be making.

**Alex:** We've really got a lot planned. At least you have some idea of the questions Ms. Garsky might ask.

**Grayson:** Yeah! Thanks a lot for helping me to plan ahead. I'd better get going. See you later.

| | |
|---|---|
| **Number of Characters:** | 4 |
| **Character Description:** | Chuck—A teenager |
| | Dick—A teenager |
| | Mr. Burnett—The principal |
| | Ms. Line—The secretary |
| **Scene Description:** | After a class discussion about student rights, Chuck decides to talk to Mr. Burnett, the principal. |

**Marty:** That was a good discussion we had today. I had no idea we had so many rights.

**Chuck:** Yeah, but look at how many rights we don't have! We always have teachers supervising us. They tell us how loud to talk, where to stand, what to look like. I'm sick of it!

**Marty:** Settle down. Don't get so hyper.

**Chuck:** How can I settle down? We should be able to do so many things in this school and we can't! I've got a study period next hour. I'm going to talk to the principal.

**Marty:** What are you going to talk about?

**Chuck:** Our rights, of course! We should have more. Do you want to come with me?

**Marty:** No, I have math next hour.

*[Chuck walks into the school office.]*

**Ms. Line:** Can I help you?

**Chuck:** Is Mr. Burnett in? I'd like to see him.

**Ms. Line:** Yes, he's in. I'll let him know you are waiting.

---

**Chuck:** Thank you.

*[Ms. Line tells Mr. Burnett that Chuck is waiting to see him.]*

**Mr. Burnett:** I understand you want to see me. Come into my office.

*[Bill enters Mr. Burnett's office and sits down.]*

**Mr. Burnett:** What can I do for you?

**Chuck:** We just had a discussion in our communications class about student rights. I feel that we don't have enough rights in this school.

**Mr. Burnett:** Well, what rights do you think you should have?

**Chuck:** *[Nervously]* You know . . . ah . . . more rights!

*[Chuck is so nervous, he forgets the rights he has been telling Marty about.]*

**Mr. Burnett:** You've told me that already. You get your ideas organized. Plan out what you want to say. Maybe you should make a list. When you've thought this out, then come back to see me.

**Chuck:** I'll do that. Thanks a lot.

*[Chuck leaves and sees his friend, Marty.]*

**Marty:** Well, what happened?

**Chuck:** I told him I thought we should have more rights.

**Marty:** Boy, you've got more guts than I have! What did he say?

**Chuck:** He said to plan out what rights I'm talking about. He said to make a list. After I get a plan, he told me to come back to see him.

**Marty:** Are you going to do it?

**Chuck:** Maybe. Let's get to class.

# Skill 15 — Receiving a Compliment

**Definition of Skill:** Accepting positive comments about oneself or about one's accomplishments

**Skill Activities/ Discussions:**

1. Discuss what a *compliment* is. Discuss the different feelings people have when they are given a compliment (e.g., pride, embarrassment).

2. Brainstorm with the class lists of appropriate and inappropriate ways to accept a compliment.

3. Discuss the consequences of accepting a compliment inappropriately.

**Situations:**

**Home**
The final grades for the year came out. Your hard work paid off. Your dad complimented you on your good grades. Accept the compliment appropriately.

**School**
A friend complimented you on your new clothes. Accept the compliment appropriately.

**Community**
An older lady dropped her groceries all over the sidewalk. After you helped her pick them up, she paid you a compliment. Demonstrate how you would accept the compliment.

| | |
|---|---|
| **Number of Characters:** | 4 |
| **Character Description:** | Mr. Furst—The coach |
| | Mitchell—A runner |
| | John—A friend |
| | Sherry—A friend |
| **Scene Description:** | Mitchell is a runner. He has the biggest run of his life coming up. He has been training hard for it. The scene begins when Mitchell and John have just finished training. |

**John:** You did a super job on that mile run.

**Mitchell:** Thanks! I felt good. I just hope I can do as well at the meet on Saturday. How are you doing on your hurdling?

**John:** The coach said that my form has really improved. Now all I have to think about is picking up my time.

**Mitchell:** By the end of the season, we should all have improved on our times.

**John:** I'd better get going. See you at the meet.

*[It's shortly before the meet begins, and the coach walks up to Mitchell.]*

**Mr. Furst:** Now, Mitchell, you can take it all. You're the best miler we have. You keep that in mind, and get out there and do your best.

**Mitchell:** Thanks for the encouragement. I feel real good, Coach. I'll try.

*[The race is over and Mitchell has won.]*

**Mr. Furst:** Super job, Mitchell! Your hard work while training paid off! You will be setting records by the end of the season.

**Mitchell:** Thanks a lot, Coach. I really appreciate everything you've done for me.

**Sherry:** Way to go, Mitchell! You sure smoked them during the last leg of the race. I don't think I'll ever forget how you left them in the dust! Someday, I'll be bragging about how I know you. You're going to the Olympics. I know you will.

**Mitchell:** It's great to have friends like you bragging me up! Without you and the others on the team always encouraging me, I don't think I could have done it. Thanks a lot.

**Number of Characters:** 4

**Character Description:** Paula—A friend of the singers

Meg—A singer

Steve—A singer

Lisa—A singer

**Scene Description:** Meg, Steve, and Lisa just sang in the student talent show. The scene begins when Paula walks up to them after their performance.

**Paula:** *[Rushing up to Meg, Steve, and Lisa]* You were tremendous! You are good enough to make a recording.

**Meg:** Do you really think so? Didn't you hear how flat I was in the second verse?

**Steve:** Who do you think you're kidding, Paula? You don't know music very well if you think we are good.

**Lisa:** Thanks for the compliment. Now, what do you want? Every time somebody says something nice to me, they want something. What is it that you want?

**Paula:** I don't want anything! I just wanted to let you know that I thought you sounded really good. But the next time you sing, I won't bother. First, you tell me I don't know anything, and then you think I want something from you.

**Steve:** Hey, don't get us wrong. We . . .

**Paula:** It's you three who have things wrong. Don't you know what to say when someone gives you a compliment? You'd better learn!

*[Paula walks away.]*

# Skill 16 Giving a Compliment

**Definition of Skill:** Making comments that acknowledge positive aspects about a person or his or her accomplishments

**Skill Activities/ Discussions:**

1. Discuss when a compliment should be given. Discuss how compliments make people feel.

2. Make "compliments" posters. Put each student's name on a sheet of paper (one name per page). Put the papers around the room. Have the students walk around the room, writing a compliment on each person's sheet. When everyone has written one compliment to each student, give each student his or her sheet.

3. Have the students keep a "compliment journal" for one week. Have students record who compliments were given to and under what circumstances.

**Situations:**

**Home**

Your parents sent you to the grocery store down the street. You are struggling to carry two bags of groceries. A friend, who is always nice, offers to help you carry one bag. Compliment that person for the assistance.

**School**

One of your friends bought a new CD player. It's almost the best you have ever heard. Compliment your friend.

**Community**

Your favorite waitress is waiting on your table in a restaurant. She always does a good job. Give her a compliment.

| | |
|---|---|
| **Number of Characters:** | 3 |
| **Character Description:** | Serena—A friend |
| | Jane—A friend |
| | Mr. Carne—The teacher |
| **Scene Description:** | Serena and Jane are trying out for the same part in a play. This scene takes place during and after their tryouts. |

**Serena:** Gosh, I was nervous when I was going through the scene. My heart was pounding.

**Jane:** You sure could have fooled me. I had no idea you were nervous. I wonder when Mr. Carne is going to call me up to read.

**Mr. Carne:** Jane, will you please come up?

**Jane:** I guess I don't have to wonder when I'm going to be called anymore.

*[After Jane's reading is finished . . .]*

**Serena:** Jane, you did a great job! Even though I want that part, I hope you get it. You really made me believe you were the character you were playing.

**Jane:** Thanks. I was so nervous! It seemed to me like I was going to explode!

**Mr. Carne:** I've looked my notes over and have concluded that Jane will get the part.

**Serena:** I'm so happy for you! You deserved it! Maybe I'll get a different part.

**Jane:** Thanks, Serena. I hope you get a different part, too!

**Mr. Carne:** And the part of Annie will go to Serena Marrero!

**Jane:** Serena, that's great! We can practice together!

| | |
|---|---|
| **Number of Characters:** | 3 |
| **Character Description:** | Miguel—A friend |
| | Ray—A friend |
| | Maria—A friend |
| **Scene Description:** | Maria and Miguel have been dating for several months. Miguel and Ray go to watch Maria perform in a roller-blading show. It is the first show in which Maria has ever skated. |

**Ray:** Look at that triple spin! Maria is really good!

**Miguel:** I wouldn't say real good. She is better than I am, I guess.

**Ray:** What do you mean, *better than you*? Neither one of us could ever be as good as she is!

**Miguel:** I just meant that she is OK.

**Ray:** Miguel, don't you appreciate what you've got? Maria is great to look at and she is talented to boot! Her performance is over. She's coming over to see us.

**Maria:** Hi, Miguel.

**Ray:** Maria, you really are good. Thanks for inviting me.

**Maria:** I'm glad you and Miguel came. It's always nice to have friends in the audience. Well, Miguel, what did you think?

**Miguel:** What do you mean?

**Maria:** I mean what do you think of the show?

**Miguel:** It's different.

**Maria:** *[Looking hurt]* Different?

**Miguel:** Well, I've never been to a roller-blading show like this before.

---

**Maria:** [_Sadly_] I guess I forgot. I've got to change. I'll see you by the front door.

[_Maria skates off._]

**Miguel:** Maria sure got sad all of a sudden. I wonder why?

**Ray:** Miguel, you dope! Don't you know why she is sad?

**Miguel:** No.

**Ray:** She wanted you to say something nice to her about the show. And all you could say was that it was _different_.

**Miguel:** I didn't mean anything bad by saying different. I just meant that I'm not used to these kinds of shows.

**Ray:** You had better wise up, man! You're going to lose that girl if you don't say anything nice to her.

**Miguel:** It's hard for me to do that.

**Ray:** Well, you had better start. Once in a while, a person has to hear something nice!

## Skill 17 — Saying Thank You

**Definition of Skill:** Expressing appreciation to someone who has done something nice

**Skill Activities/ Discussions:**

1. Have students tell about a time when they said "thank you" to someone and why.

2. Have the students brainstorm and develop a list of nice things that students do for each other during the school day (other than give a compliment).

3. Ask students to write down the last nice thing they did for someone else and whether or not they received a thank you. Discuss how people feel when they get a thank you and how they feel when they do not.

4. Discuss what could happen if people never said thank you to others who did nice things for them.

**Situations:**

**Home**
You are getting picked up for a movie in five minutes, and you still have to blow dry your hair and iron your shirt. You brother offers to iron it for you. Demonstrate how you would express your appreciation.

**School**
Your teacher stayed at school until 5:00 helping you study for a test. Show how you would say thank you.

**Community**
Someone has given you directions to the service counter in a big store. Express your appreciation.

## Script A — Saying Thank You

| | |
|---|---|
| **Number of Characters:** | 3 |
| **Character Description:** | Joy—A teenager |
| | Lee—Joy's older brother |
| | Mrs. Oh—Joy and Lee's mother |
| **Scene Description:** | Lee, who has been away all year at a technical school, has just come back home for the summer. The scene begins when Joy, Lee, and Mrs. Oh are finishing up with their evening meal. |

**Mrs. Oh:** *[Looking at Lee]* Why don't you and Joy go for a walk? I'll take care of the dishes tonight. You two probably have a lot of catching up to do.

*[Joy looks relieved to get out of doing the dishes.]*

**Lee:** That sounds like a good idea; except, we'll do the dishes first, and then we'll start the walk. How does that sound Joy?

**Joy:** *[Looking disappointed]* OK, I guess.

**Lee:** Thanks for the great supper; it's my favorite.

**Mrs. Oh:** Well, you're welcome. It's nice to have you home again. If you two do the dishes, then I'll go start the laundry. Do you both have all your dirty clothes in the hamper?

**Joy:** I think so.

**Lee:** I do, too! Thank you. I can't tell you how much I appreciate that. I felt like I spent half my freshman year at the laundromat.

*[Joy and Lee walk into the kitchen to start the dishes.]*

**Joy:** I'm glad you're home. It's been really different around here with you gone.

**Lee:** Thanks for saying so. I'm glad to be back and I've missed you, too!

**Joy:** There you go again with the thank yous. What's with you?

**Lee:** What?

**Joy:** Ever since you walked in the door, you've been saying, "Thank you this, thank you that."

**Lee:** Oh, that's what you mean. I'll tell you. Things were really different for me this year. All of a sudden everything was up to me. I did my own laundry, my own shopping, my own mending, my own everything.

**Joy:** Sounds rough!

**Lee:** It was, especially at first. You know, I never used to thank Mom for any of the things she did for me. I just decided I should start thanking her every once in a while.

**Joy:** Come to think of it, I never thank her either.

*[Joy and Lee finish the dishes and go for a walk.]*

| | |
|---|---|
| **Number of Characters:** | 3 |
| **Character Description:** | Mr. Chin—Noriko's father |
| | Noriko—A teenager |
| | Mr. Wilson—An elderly person |
| **Scene Description:** | The scene begins when Mr. Chin and Noriko are getting into their car in the parking ramp at the mall. |

**Mr. Chin:** What a madhouse! The mall was packed today.

**Noriko:** Must be all those 4th of July sales. No wonder we had to park so far up.

**Mr. Chin:** Do you see our car?

**Noriko:** Yeah, it's up there on the left.

*[Just then, Noriko and her dad notice an elderly man getting out of his car. His dog jumps out too and starts darting in between all the cars.]*

**Noriko:** Dad, are we in any real hurry? I'd like to help that man catch his dog.

**Mr. Chin:** That's really a nice idea. He looks like he could use the help. Here, I'll take the packages.

*[Noriko takes off after the dog while Mr. Wilson stands yelling for the animal to come back. Noriko almost catches it behind a red truck, but it gets away again. Mr. Chin can see Noriko turn the corner after the dog and then both are out of sight. Mr. Chin walks over to Mr. Wilson and tries to get him to stop yelling.]*

**Mr. Chin:** Hello, my name is Mr. Chin. Don't worry, my daughter is pretty fast. You'll have your dog back in no time.

**Mr. Wilson:** That darn dog! I should know better than to bring it along in the car.

---

*[Mr. Chin notices Noriko walking up with the dog in her arms and doesn't know who is more out of breath, the dog or Noriko!]*

**Noriko:**　Here's your dog. Cute little guy and fast, too!

**Mr. Wilson:**　You bad dog, taking off like that!

*[Mr. Wilson puts the dog in the car, turns around and walks to the elevator without saying thank you.]*

**Mr. Chin:**　I can't believe he just walked away without saying anything to you!

**Noriko:**　No kidding! I darn near killed myself chasing that dog!

**Mr. Chin:**　It was awfully nice for you to help that man, but I imagine it took part of the fun away when he didn't express his appreciation.

**Noriko:**　You're right.

**Skill 18**     **Introducing Yourself**

**Definition of Skill:**    Telling someone your name when you meet for the first time

**Skill Activities/ Discussions:**

1. Have students think of several situations when they would need to introduce themselves (e.g., when meeting a new student at school, checking in at the reception desk, when getting a haircut).

2. Discuss situations when they would not want to give someone their name.

3. Talk about strategies to help people remember a name when they are introduced to someone.

**Situations:**    **Home**

Your older sister's date is waiting for her in the living room. Introduce yourself to him.

**School**

You have been sent to escort a guest speaker to the auditorium. Introduce yourself to her.

**Community**

You need to let the receptionist know you have arrived for your dental appointment. Introduce yourself to her.

| | |
|---|---|
| **Number of Characters:** | 3 |
| **Character Description:** | Marta—A teenager |
| | Mr. Segura—Marta's father |
| | Mrs. Hempfer—A neighbor |
| **Scene Description:** | The scene begins when Marta is just about ready to leave for a baby-sitting job. |

**Mr. Segura:** What time are you getting picked up to baby-sit?

**Marta:** At 8:00, but I'll walk because it's just four houses down, at the new neighbor's.

**Mr. Segura:** Oh, at the Hempfer's house? Have you met them before?

**Marta:** No. I guess they have one little boy who is two years old.

**Mr. Segura:** How did they hear about you?

**Marta:** I guess the Jacksons referred me to them.

**Mr. Segura:** How nice! Since you've only spoken to them over the phone, remember to introduce yourself when they answer the door. You may even want to take your baby-sitting certificate along with you.

**Marta:** I've got it in my backpack. I'd better get going. See you later.

**Mr. Segura:** How late will you be?

**Marta:** I'm not sure. I'll call you when I find out.

*[Marta walks up to the Hempfer's front door and rings the door bell. Mrs. Hempfer answers it.]*

**Mrs. Hempfer:** Hello!

**Marta:** Hello, Mrs. Hempfer. My name is Marta. I'm here to baby-sit for your son.

**Mrs. Hempfer:** Well, come right on in. It's nice to meet you. The Jacksons have nothing but good things to say about you. Here is the number where we can be reached. We should be home before 10:00. Don't hesitate to call if you need anything.

*[Mrs Hempfer shows Marta around the house and stops outside her son's bedroom.]*

**Mrs. Hempfer:** I was hoping Timmy would still be awake so I could introduce you to him, but he was just too tired and fell asleep. He probably won't wake up at all, but just in case, we told him you were coming.

*[Not 15 minutes after the Hempfers leave, Timmy comes out of his room.]*

**Marta:** Hi, Timmy! My name is Marta. Remember, your mommy and daddy told you I would be here tonight? How would you like me to read you a book until they get back?

*[Timmy nods his head yes. He is back to sleep before Marta finishes two pages.]*

| | |
|---|---|
| **Number of Characters:** | 3 |
| **Character Description:** | Joel—A teenager |
| | Mr. Thunder—Joel's father |
| | Jake—Joel's friend |
| **Scene Description** | The scene begins when Joel is just sitting down to do homework. He remembers the history assignment to read Chapter 12, but discovers that he left the book at Jake's house. Joel goes to the garage to find his dad. |

**Joel:** Dad, I've got to go back over to Jake's house. I left my history book over there, and I'm supposed to read Chapter 12 for tomorrow.

**Mr. Thunder:** That's too bad. Why not call first to make sure someone is home?

*[Joel goes into the family room to make the call. The phone rings four times and then he hears the following message: "Hello, no one at the Klein residence is available to come to the phone right now. If you wish to speak to any of us, please say who you want to talk to and give your name and number at the sound of the beep. We'll get back to you as soon as possible." Joel freezes because he has never gotten a message like that before.]*

**Joel:** Oh . . . please call me when you get home.

*[Joel hangs up quickly and goes back to the garage.]*

**Joel:** I had to leave a message on their answering machine. Man, that really made me nervous.

**Mr. Thunder:** I know what you mean. Those things always catch me off guard too.

*[Joel waits all night for Jake to return his call, but never hears from him. The next day at school, Joel goes to Jake's locker.]*

**Joel:** Hi, Jake!

**Jake:** Hi, Joel! Am ever tired today! I was up late reading that history assignment. Did you get it all read?

**Joel:** No, I didn't. I think I set my history book in your garage when I left on my bike. I called you for it, but no one was home. Why didn't you return my call?

**Jake:** Was that you? We couldn't figure out who called. You forgot to give your name or tell who you were calling for. I couldn't even recognize your voice.

**Joel:** *[Laughing]* So that's why! I've never left a message on an answering machine before.

**Jake:** They take a little getting used to. Don't feel bad. We get a lot of messages where people forget to introduce themselves. I'm sorry you couldn't get your history read.

**Joel:** I guess all I can do now is go and explain everything to the teacher. I'll see you later. Bye.

**Jake:** Bye, Joel.

| Skill | **19** | **Introducing Others** |

**Definition of Skill:** Helping two people who do not know each other to learn each other's names

**Skill Activities/ Discussions:**

1. Discuss the different language used when making formal and informal introductions.

2. Discuss what should be done when students are not sure whether they need to introduce two people to each other who may not have met before.

3. Invite the school principal and vice-principal into the class so that students can practice making formal introductions.

**Situations:**

**Home**

You are bringing a new friend over to your house. Show how you would introduce your friend and one of your parents to each other.

**School**

Your cousin is visiting your family and goes to school with you on Friday. Demonstrate how you would introduce your cousin to your teachers.

**Community**

You and a friend are shopping and run into a person for whom you baby-sit. Introduce the two of them to each other.

| | |
|---|---|
| **Number of Characters:** | 4 |
| **Character Description:** | Ida—A student |
| | Mrs. Carson—Ida's mother |
| | Bev—A friend |
| | Ms. Waldo—The teacher |
| **Scene Description:** | The scene begins with Ida and Bev talking to each other on the phone. |

**Bev:** So you're really going along with your mom to parent-teacher conferences tonight?

**Ida:** Yeah, I used to get all upset as a little kid when my parents went by themselves to conferences. I used to think they weren't telling me everything. So, they started taking me with them.

**Bev:** Not me! I never want to know what they find out at those meetings.

**Ida:** I'll tell you one thing. I'm pretty good at making introductions.

**Bev:** I bet you are! Well, I'll give you credit. You've really got guts!

**Ida:** You'd be surprised. It's not bad. All the teachers do is tell you what things you're good at, what things you could improve on, and what your grade is so far.

**Mrs. Carson:** Come on, Ida. Our first conference is in 15 minutes.

**Ida:** Bye, Bev! I gotta get going. See you tomorrow.

*[Mrs. Carson and Ida head off to school. Their first conference is with Ms. Waldo, the science teacher. They take a seat outside her room and wait for their turn.]*

**Ms. Waldo:** Well, hello, Ida! I didn't know you were joining us tonight. I'm glad you came.

---

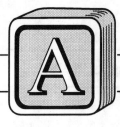

**Ida:** Ms. Waldo, I'd like to introduce you to my mother, Mrs. Carson. Mom, this is Ms. Waldo, my science teacher.

**Mrs. Carson:** Hello.

**Ms. Waldo:** It's a pleasure to meet you, Mrs. Carson. I've enjoyed having your daughter in my class this year. Come on in and have a seat. I'll show you some of the work we've been doing so far this year.

| | |
|---|---|
| **Number of Characters:** | 3 |
| **Character Description:** | Maurice—A teenager |
| | Jack—A teenager |
| | Paula—A teenager |
| **Scene Description:** | Jack moved into Maurice's neighborhood during the summer and will be going to Maurice's school next year. The scene begins when Maurice and Jack are at the beach together. |

**Jack:** So, what's your school like? I want to know what to expect next fall.

**Maurice:** It's pretty cool. The principal is strict and nobody gets away with much, but the kids are great! And there's a lot of clubs and stuff.

*[Maurice recognizes a friend from school and calls out, "Hello."]*

**Maurice:** Our girls' and guys' teams are pretty good. Are you into any sports?

**Jack:** I'll probably try out for basketball. How about you?

*[Maurice sees another friend and waves.]*

**Maurice:** Cross-country is my sport.

**Jack:** Man, it seems like you know everyone here at the beach. Leaving all my friends was the hardest part about moving. I'm glad we met right away.

**Maurice:** Me, too! Wait till school starts, and you'll meet all sorts of other people.

*[Paula notices Maurice and walks up to say, "Hi."]*

**Maurice:** Hi, Paula! Where have you been? I haven't seen you all summer!

**Paula:** My family took a trip for four weeks. We just got back yesterday. It was fun, but I'm glad to be back.

*[Jack was eager to be introduced to someone new.]*

**Maurice:**    Have you talked to Juanda or Jim at all? I haven't seen them at all.

*[Paula looks at Jack and wonders who he is.]*

**Paula:**    No. Maybe I'll give them a call tonight and catch up.

**Maurice:**    Where did you go on your trip?

*[Jack starts to feel a little left out.]*

**Paula:**    All over! We stopped at Disneyland. That was a blast! Oh, there's my mom to pick me up. I'll call later.

**Maurice:**    OK. Bye!

*[Paula walks away.]*

**Jack:**    Who was that?

**Maurice:**    That was Paula. You'll meet her at school.

**Jack:**    I wanted to meet her now.

**Maurice:**    Oh, no! Am I ever dumb! I'm sorry, I wasn't thinking.

**Jack:**    That's OK. Want to go in the water?

**Maurice:**    Good idea! I'm really hot!

## Skill 20 — Offering Help

**Definition of Skill:** Offering assistance to someone who is in need

**Skill Activities/ Discussions:**

1. Have students tell about the last time they offered to help someone.

2. Discuss situations where students are not sure whether to offer help or not; for example, to a blind person, or a person in a wheelchair, or an elderly person. Discuss what makes those situations so difficult.

3. Discuss the difference between offering help and "taking over."

**Situations:**

**Home**

Your younger brother is struggling with his very first word search puzzle. Demonstrate how you could offer to help in a nice way, without making him feel stupid.

**School**

You sit next to a student in science class who has trouble taking notes. Offer to help him by sharing your notes, without making him feel bad.

**Community**

You notice a woman struggling in the parking lot because she is trying to get two small children and a bag of groceries to her car. Demonstrate how you could offer to help.

| | |
|---|---|
| **Number of Characters:** | 3 |
| **Character Description:** | Clair—A teenager |
| | Theo—Clair's younger brother |
| | Mr. Murphy—Clair and Theo's dad |
| **Scene Description:** | The scene begins with Clair and her dad talking in the kitchen. |

| | |
|---|---|
| **Clair:** | Where is Theo? |
| **Mr. Murphy:** | Downstairs, doing homework. |
| **Clair:** | Schoolwork? I didn't think they had to bring stuff home at that age. I've got so much homework now, sometimes I wish I was young again. |
| **Mr. Murphy:** | Theo's teacher, Mr. Olson, gave the kids their first homework assignment for the year. |
| **Clair:** | Oh, yeah? What kind of homework? |
| **Mr. Murphy:** | Math. Theo was so excited when he came home from school. He felt so grown up. Theo said to me, "I have to add and take away. I better get right to work on it before we eat!" |

*[Mr. Murphy and Clair both smile.]*

| | |
|---|---|
| **Mr. Murphy:** | There is one problem, though. I just went to check on him, and he is having some problems. |
| **Clair:** | Did you get him straightened out? |
| **Mr. Murphy:** | Well, no! I offered to help, but Theo said no. He is in that stage where he wants to do everything independently. |
| **Clair:** | Think maybe I should give it a try? |

**Mr. Murphy:** Would you? Maybe it's easier to receive help from a sister than it is from a parent. Just approach the subject carefully.

**Clair:** Wish me luck.

*[Clair goes into Theo's bedroom.]*

**Clair:** Hi, Theo! I came in to tell you we'll be ready to eat soon.

**Theo:** *[In a depressed voice]* OK. I'll be up soon.

**Clair:** Math homework, I see. I have to do some math tonight myself, only mine is on fractions. I always have such a hard time with fractions. Sometimes I feel like I'll never understand it.

**Theo:** Oh, yeah? Mine is add and take away.

**Clair:** I had a hard time with that too when I was first learning it.

**Theo:** I'm having trouble with the whole thing!

**Clair:** If you don't mind, maybe I could work the first couple of problems with you and then you could do the rest yourself.

**Theo:** You won't tell Mom or Dad?

**Clair:** No way! Let's have a look at number one. Oh, these are hard ones!

| | |
|---|---|
| **Number of Characters:** | 4 |
| **Character Description:** | Bob—A teenager |
| | Mr. Perez—Kids' Club Teacher |
| | Kim—A young club member |
| | Rafael—An older club member |
| **Scene Description:** | Mr. Perez needs some extra help on the big Christmas Craft project he has planned for the Kids' Club members. Bob has volunteered to go along with Mr. Perez to the meeting to be an assistant. The scene begins when Mr. Perez and Bob are setting up before the kids arrive. |

**Bob:** So what exactly are the kids going to be making with all this stuff?

**Mr. Perez:** A wreath.

*[Mr. Perez shows Bob an example.]*

**Mr. Perez:** This is what it looks like. I'll be telling the kids how to make it, right after everyone gets here.

**Bob:** Will they be able to finish it today?

**Mr. Perez:** Most of them will. They really enjoy craft projects.

**Bob:** What would you like me to do when the kids are working?

**Mr. Perez:** Why don't you walk around to all the kids to see if anyone needs help? I'm sure there will be lots of questions, especially with the younger kids.

**Bob:** Sounds good!

**Mr. Perez:** I really appreciate your help, Bob! I don't think I would have been able to set up on time without you.

*[At 3:00, the kids start coming in and find a place to sit. They all like the wreath and can hardly wait for the leader to finish giving directions, so they can get started. When the kids get under way, the questions start rolling in and Mr. Perez and Bob are very busy. Bob notices a young girl having a difficult time trying to glue a pine cone on her wreath. It keeps falling off. He goes over to help her.]*

**Bob:** Here, Kim, let me get that.

*[Bob takes the pine cone and glues it on for Kim. She suddenly starts to cry.]*

**Bob:** What's wrong?

**Kim:** *[Sobbing]* That's not where I wanted it!

**Rafael:** That's what you get for grabbing it away from her!

**Bob:** It looked like Kim was having such a hard time, I just wanted to help.

**Rafael:** Why didn't you ask her if she wanted help?

**Bob:** I see what you mean! Here, Kim, I'll take it off. You can put it back on where you'd like it to be.

## Skill 21 — Asking for Help

| | |
|---|---|
| **Definition of Skill:** | Letting other people know about difficulties and asking for their assistance |

**Skill Activities/ Discussions:**

1. List different situations when teenagers may need help, and from whom they could get the help.

2. Ask students to tell about a time when they did not ask for help, but found out they should have.

3. Discuss why it is sometimes difficult to ask for help.

**Situations:**

**Home**

You get into some trouble with your friends. Demonstrate how you could ask your older brother or sister to help you solve your problem.

**School**

You are having a difficult time finishing the decorations for the school dance. Demonstrate how you would ask your friends to help you finish after school.

**Community**

You are having difficulty finding a certain book. Demonstrate how you would ask the public librarian to help you use the *Readers' Guide*.

| | |
|---|---|
| **Number of Characters:** | 4 |
| **Character Description:** | Jesse—A teenager |
| | Mr. Hermesen—Jesse's father |
| | Ms. Sanchez—Jesse's boss |
| | Julie—Jesse's coworker |
| **Scene Description:** | Jesse is in the garage getting his bike out because he has to be to work in a half-hour. The scene begins when Mr. Hermesen pulls into the garage. |

| | |
|---|---|
| **Mr. Hermesen:** | Not bad. What did you do today? |
| **Jesse:** | We went to play tennis this morning. |
| **Mr. Hermesen:** | Looks like you're just about ready to leave for work. |
| **Jesse:** | Yeah, my shift starts at 5:00. I think I work the cash register again today. I'm beginning to get the hang of it. |
| **Mr. Hermesen:** | Hey! Did I tell you I ran into your boss downtown yesterday? |
| **Jesse:** | Ms. Sanchez? No, you didn't. |
| **Mr. Hermesen:** | She had a lot of good things to say about you. |
| **Jesse:** | Get out of here! She did not! |
| **Mr. Hermesen:** | She really did! She said you work very independently and handle things on your own. She told me about last week, when the register ran out of paper. Instead of asking her how to change it, you looked it up in the manual, and did it yourself. I'm really proud of you. |
| **Jesse:** | *[In a joking voice]* Well, what can I say? When you got it, you got it! I better get going, Dad. I'll be off around 9:00. See you later! |

**Mr. Hermesen:**     Bye, Jesse.

> *[When Jesse arrives at work, he sees Ms. Sanchez busy working at her desk. He quickly punches in and relieves the clerk at Register #2. About 10 minutes later, the cash register jams up.]*

**Jesse:**     Hey, Julie. Have you ever gotten one of these jams before? I can't find anything in this manual about it.

**Julie:**     No, I haven't. You better do something quickly, though. Look at the backup in your line!

> *[Jesse thought about the compliment Ms. Sanchez had given him about doing things on his own, but he decided it was time to ask Ms. Sanchez for help.]*

**Jesse:**     Excuse me, Ms. Sanchez. I'm sorry to bother you, but I need your help with Register #2.

**Ms. Sanchez:**     It's no bother at all, Jesse. I'm sorry. I should have told you that once in a while a machine does this. I'll fix it. I'm glad you came to ask for help.

> *[Ms. Sanchez shows Jesse how to get the register unjammed. Soon, Jesse is waiting on customers again.]*

| | |
|---|---|
| **Number of Characters:** | 3 |
| **Character Description:** | Mrs. Kim—The typing teacher |
| | Kisha—A typing student |
| | Rebicca—Kisha's friend |
| **Scene Description:** | The beginning typing students have taken their second test of the semester. The scene begins when the teacher, Mrs. Kim, is handing back the tests. |

**Mrs. Kim:** I'd like you all to double-check my work by recounting the points you earned on the test. Also, grades will be coming out in two weeks, and we will only have one more test before that. If you are not happy with the grade you received on this test, please ask me for help. I'm here every day after school until 4:30. This room is also available for practice during third hour.

*[The bell rings and the students pack up and leave.*
*Kisha finds her friend, Rebicca, out in the hall.]*

**Rebicca:** Hi, Kisha! How did typing go today?

**Kisha:** Not too great! We got our tests back today and I didn't do very well.

**Rebicca:** I'm sorry, Kisha. I know you really needed to do well on that test.

**Kisha:** I do all right on the typing part. It's the written work, like figuring out margins, that I just don't understand.

**Rebicca:** I've heard Mrs. Kim is really nice. I see her helping kids all the time after school. Have you asked her for help?

**Kisha:** No, I don't want to have to do that.

**Rebicca:** Well, I know you don't have anything going on after school, now that the volleyball season is over. And it's not like you have to catch a bus. Why not get some help?

**Kisha:** Look, almost everyone else thinks that margins are easy to figure out. If I ask for help, then they will know I don't understand it.

**Rebicca:** If I were you, I wouldn't let that bother me. Suit yourself. But remember, grades are coming out soon.

*[Two weeks later, Kisha and Rebicca are eating together.]*

**Kisha:** Well, Rebicca, it looks like you were right.

**Rebicca:** About what?

**Kisha:** About asking for help in typing class. I got a "D" and now I have to try to explain to my folks why I didn't get extra help.

**Rebicca:** I'm sorry, Kisha. Sometimes it's hard to ask for help. But once you ask, you'll find out it's not so bad. I guess everybody has trouble with something. Take me, for example I have to get help from the math tutor and you think math is easy.

**Kisha:** I see what you mean.

# Skill 22 Asking Permission

**Definition of Skill:** Asking to be allowed to participate in a desired activity

**Skill Activities/ Discussions:**

1. Brainstorm and make a list of things teenagers should ask permission to do, and from whom they should ask permission.

2. Discuss why it is important to ask permission.

3. Discuss why it is sometimes difficult for teenagers, who are becoming more independent, to feel they need to ask permission.

**Situations:**

**Home**
You have saved up money and want to paint your bedroom. Demonstrate how you would ask permission from your parents.

**School**
Your cousin is visiting you and has a three-day weekend, but you don't. Demonstrate how you would ask permission from the school principal to bring your cousin to school as a visitor.

**Community**
Your neighbors own the vacant lot at the end of the block. Demonstrate how you would ask permission to use it to play softball.

| | |
|---|---|
| **Number of Characters:** | 4 |
| **Character Description:** | Larry—A teenager |
| | Kenton—A teenager |
| | Pete—A teenager |
| | Mrs. Olm—A neighbor |
| **Scene Description:** | Larry invited two of his friends to his cottage on the lake for the weekend. The scene begins when they decide to go swimming. |

**Kenton:** Wow! This place is great! I can't believe how clear the water is!

**Pete:** I wish we had a place like this.

**Larry:** Yeah, we have a lot of fun up here! The water is so clear because motors aren't allowed on the lake.

**Pete:** What a bummer! That means you can't go water-skiing or jet-skiing. I bet you wish they didn't have that rule.

**Kenton:** Of course, if motors were allowed, then your lake wouldn't be as private and clear as it is now.

**Larry:** You're both right. There definitely are pros and cons. The good news is we could go canoeing and not get swamped by the waves.

**Kenton:** Great! Let's go canoeing!

**Larry:** Well, there's one problem. We don't own a canoe. We usually borrow our neighbor's canoe, but they aren't here this weekend.

**Pete:** Do you know where they keep the canoe and paddles?

**Larry:** Yeah, out in that shed. I even know where they keep the key.

**Kenton:** We don't have a problem then. Why don't you go get the key and Pete and I will put the canoe in the water?

**Larry:** I'm not sure about this, guys. The Olms are really nice about letting us use it when they are here, but I don't feel right about doing this without their permission.

**Pete:** If they have let you use it before, why would they mind?

**Larry:** Yeah, but if something happens to the canoe, you two won't have to face them and explain like I will!

**Kenton:** I guess you're right. Let's jump in and go for a swim.

**Larry:** Hey, I've got an idea! I know the Olms live in Janesville. If you'll help pay the long-distance phone bill, I'll call and ask if we could use their boat.

**Pete:** Good thinking!

*[The three boys walk to the cabin and Larry dials the phone.]*

**Mrs. Olm:** Hello.

**Larry:** Hello, Mrs. Olm! This is Larry West speaking.

**Mrs. Olm:** Well, how are you, Larry?

**Larry:** Oh, I'm fine. Some friends and I are up at our cottage this weekend. I was wondering if we could have permission to use your canoe while we are here.

**Mrs. Olm:** I think that would be fine, Larry. You have always taken care of it when you've used it in the past. Do you remember where the key is hidden?

**Larry:** Yes, I do. Thank you very much for letting us use it. Will you be up next weekend?

**Mrs. Olm:** Yes, we will. I'm glad you called and asked permission, Larry. That shows you're responsible. I better let you go. Have fun!

**Larry:** We sure will. Good-bye.

| Number of Characters: | 3 |
|---|---|
| Character Description: | Labar—A teenager |
| | Abby—A teenager |
| | Ms. Crump—The school's vice-principal |
| Scene Description: | Labar and Abby meet at their lockers right before lunch and are talking. |

**Labar:** I could hardly stay awake last hour. I was in Room 212 and the room had to be 90°.

**Abby:** I know. I wish they could get the temperature regulated a little better around here. Hey, where is your sack lunch? Did you leave it in your locker?

**Labar:** No, I'm not going to eat today. I have to go out the back door and head to the store.

**Abby:** Are you kidding? During school hours?

**Labar:** Yeah! Today is Mr. Stramp's birthday and I forgot to get him a card. He's my favorite teacher and I want to do something for him.

**Abby:** We don't have an open campus. The only way you can leave is to bring a note from home. You better at least go to the office and ask permission.

**Labar:** No way! I'm not some kid! It's not like I'm doing anything wrong. I'm just going to get a card. Besides, I'll be gone 10 minutes max!

**Abby:** I'd still ask if I were you!

**Labar:** Yeah? Well, what if they say no? I'm old enough to make my own decisions.

*[Labar goes out the door and heads down the hill to the store. The secretary happens to be watering plants in the window and sees Labar leaving the school grounds. The secretary first checks to see if he brought in a note and then reports him to the principal. When Labar returns to school, he is called to the office.]*

**Ms. Crump:** Labar, I understand you left the school grounds during lunch.

**Labar:** Yes, I did, but it was for a good reason. Today is Mr. Stramp's birthday. I have him next hour and I wanted to get him a card.

**Ms. Crump:** I think that is very nice that you want to give him a card, but I'm afraid you've disobeyed a school policy.

**Labar:** Are you telling me that if I had asked permission beforehand, you would have let me go?

**Ms. Crump:** No, not without a note from home. But I could have given you one of these blank cards I have in my desk to use. I'm afraid I have to give you detention for leaving school.

**Labar:** Oh, come on! Can't you give me a break this time? I was trying to do something nice.

**Ms. Crump:** I know it's difficult. You are becoming an adult and you are very capable of making decisions on your own. But you need to see it from my perspective. As the vice-principal of this school, I need to know where students are at all times, in case of an emergency.

**Labar:** Man, I tried to be a nice guy, and look where it got me!

| **Skill** | **23** | **Accepting No** |

**Definition of Skill:** Going along with the decision when someone with authority says no to something you want

**Skill Activities/
Discussions:**

1. Make a list of authorities who can make yes and no decisions, such as a parent, a teacher, or a babysitter.

2. Talk about what makes no so hard to accept sometimes.

3. Discuss some of the consequences of going against a no decision from an authority.

**Situations:**

**Home**

You ask if you could see an R–rated movie with a friend and your parents say no. Demonstrate how you would accept their decision.

**School**

You ask for an extension of time to complete your English paper and your teacher says no. Show acceptance of that decision.

**Community**

You ask if you can return a pair of pants you bought on sale. The clerk says, "No returns on sale items." Demonstrate how you would react to that decision.

# Script A — Accepting No

| | |
|---|---|
| **Number of Characters:** | 2 |
| **Character Description:** | Mike—A student |
| | Mr. Mortell—The teacher |
| **Scene Description:** | Mike is in Mr. Mortell's room, talking before school on Monday morning. |

**Mike:** Good morning, Mr. Mortell!

**Mr. Mortell:** Hello, Mike! How was your weekend?

**Mike:** It was great! That's why I came in. I want to tell you about it. Are you busy?

**Mr. Mortell:** No, I've got a few minutes. Besides, now you have my curiosity up about your weekend.

**Mike:** We went to Water World. They have all the big water slides there. Man, those things are fast! On some of them, you slide through tunnels and waterfalls.

**Mr. Mortell:** Will they let anyone go on those slides?

**Mike:** Well, not the little kids. You have to be over a certain height before they will let you on.

**Mr. Mortell:** *[Looking at his watch]* Excuse me. I don't mean to interrupt, but where is your first-hour class?

**Mike:** Downstairs. Why?

**Mr. Mortell:** I just want to make sure you get there on time.

**Mike:** No problem. There's this one water slide that even I didn't go on. It's really high and it drops you almost straight down for 50 feet.

**Mr. Mortell:** I've seen that one. I wouldn't go on it either. You know, there's only three minutes until the bell rings. Maybe you better take off. We can talk more before second hour.

**Mike:** You're right. I'll see you next period.

*[Mike stops to comb his hair and then looks at the lunch menu. Mr. Mortell notices that Mike even stops for a drink of water. Sure enough, the bell rings and Mike runs down the stairs to class. Five minutes later, Mike comes back to Mr. Mortell's office.]*

**Mr. Mortell:** Late for class?

**Mike:** Yeah. I need a pass to get into class. I was wondering, since I was talking to you, and you are a teacher, could you mark it excused?

**Mr. Mortell:** No, Mike. I'm sorry, I can't. You know I enjoyed hearing about your weekend, but that's not the reason you were late. I watched you comb your hair and get a drink when you knew you only had three minutes.

**Mike:** Please? This is my third tardy and I'll get detention.

**Mr. Mortell:** I'm sorry, I can't do it, Mike. It just wouldn't be fair to the other students who take the responsibility to get to class on time.

**Mike:** How about if you excuse it just this once? I won't do it again.

**Mr. Mortell:** I can't do that, Mike. It just wouldn't be . . .

**Mike:** I know! It wouldn't be fair.

*[Mr. Mortell gives Mike a pass to get back into class. It is marked "unexcused."]*

## Script **B** Accepting No

| | |
|---|---|
| **Number of Characters:** | 3 |
| **Character Description:** | Wayne—A teenager |
| | Mrs. Winter—Wayne's mom |
| | Grandpa—Wayne's grandfather |
| **Scene Description:** | Wayne is talking to his mother in the family room and decides the time is right to ask about the camp out. |

**Wayne:** Steve and I are thinking about camping out this Saturday night.

**Mrs. Winter:** That sounds like fun. Whose house are you going to stay at? Our back yard is nice and big!

**Wayne:** Camping out in a back yard is OK, but we want to stay out on the island at the beach.

**Mrs. Winter:** I'm afraid it's illegal to camp on the island.

**Wayne:** Oh, come on! I hear lots of people stay out there.

**Mrs. Winter:** I might consider letting you two stay out at the campground where there are guards on duty. But the island? I'm sorry, Wayne. It's out of the question.

**Wayne:** You never let me do anything. You always treat me like a baby.

**Mrs. Winter:** I know you're disappointed, Wayne, but I'm sorry.

*[Wayne stomps out of the family room and runs into Grandpa.]*

**Grandpa:** Hey, where are you running off to?

**Wayne:** I don't know and I don't care.

**Grandpa:** What's got you all worked up?

**Wayne:** Mom, that's what! Steve and I were going to camp out at the island this Saturday, but no, it's too dangerous.

**Grandpa:** You know your mom trusts you. There are a lot of crazy people around these days.

**Wayne:** If there are so many crazy people out there, maybe I should just lock myself in my room for the rest of my life. It's nice and safe in there.

**Grandpa:** You know your mom said no because she doesn't want to see you get hurt.

**Wayne:** No, it's because she doesn't think I can handle anything.

*[Wayne runs into his room and locks the door.]*

## Skill 24    Making an Apology

**Definition of Skill:**    Saying you are sorry

**Skill Activities/ Discussions:**

1. Pass out a list of situations in which one person must apologize to others. Include some situations that do not require an apology. Have the students identify which situations require an apology. Also instruct the students to identify who is responsible for making the apology and for what reason.

2. Discuss the reasons why making any apology may be difficult to do.

3. Ask students to provide examples of times when they had to apologize. Have them discuss how the apology was made and how they felt when making it.

**Situations:**

**Home**
You took your brother's best shirt without asking. You accidentally spilled grape juice on it. The juice won't come out. Apologize to your brother.

**School**
You accused your teacher of losing your math assignment. Actually, you forgot to turn it in. Apologize to your teacher for the accusation.

**Community**
You are working as a clerk in a clothing store. When you are with a customer, you get called to the front desk. Apologize to the customer for keeping him or her waiting when you come back.

| | |
|---|---|
| **Number of Characters:** | 3 |
| **Character Description:** | Melody—A friend |
| | Angie—A friend |
| | Jim—A friend |
| **Scene Description:** | Angie borrowed Melody's watch at the beach because she had to be home by 8 p.m. |

**Angie:** Oh, darn it! I forgot my watch at home. I have to be home at eight because I have to baby-sit.

**Melody:** If you want, you can borrow my watch and return it before you leave the beach.

**Angie:** Thanks! I appreciate the loan. Hey, Jim. How's the water?

**Jim:** It's great, especially on such a hot day!

**Angie:** Do you want to go back in?

**Jim:** Let's go!

*[A little while later . . .]*

**Jim:** I didn't know your watch was waterproof.

**Angie:** My watch! Oh, no!

**Jim:** What's wrong?

**Angie:** I borrowed Melody's watch before I went swimming. I totally forgot I had it on. I'll bet it's ruined! It's not ticking anymore!

**Jim:** There's Melody over there. You had better tell her.

**Angie:** Oh, Melody, I've got some bad news. Without thinking, I went swimming with your watch on. I'm afraid I've ruined it. I'm sorry.

**Melody:** What can I say? It was just an inexpensive watch.

**Angie:** I'd like to replace it for you. I have some money saved up. Where did you buy it?

**Melody:** Thanks, Angie. I really do need a watch. I bought it at Klein's Five-and-Ten.

**Angie:** I'll go there tomorrow. I'm sorry.

# Script **B** Making an Apology

| | |
|---|---|
| **Number of Characters:** | 3 |
| **Character Description:** | Robin—Andy's sister |
| | Andy—Robin's brother |
| | Mom—Robin and Andy's mother |
| **Scene Description:** | Robin borrowed her older brother Andy's ten-speed bike. |

**Andy:**   Hi, Robin! I'm just going out for a bike ride. Do you want to come?

**Robin:**   A bike ride! No, I don't want to come. Are you sure you want to go for a bike ride?

**Andy:**   Yes, I'm sure. Boy, you sure are acting strange. Of course, I forgot that you're strange to begin with! *[Begins laughing]*

**Robin:**   Let's play Ping-Pong instead. Or how about shooting hoops before we eat dinner?

**Andy:**   What's wrong? You sure don't want to go for a bike ride.

**Robin:**   I'm sick. I don't feel well.

**Andy:**   But you feel well enough to do everything else. What's wrong? I'm going for a bike ride.

**Robin:**   No, you can't!

**Andy:**   Why can't I?

**Robin:**   You're not going to get mad, are you?

**Andy:**   I'm going to get really mad if you don't tell me what's going on!

**Robin:**   You know how crowded the garage is?

**Andy:**   Yeah.

**Robin:**   Well, your bike happened to be in front and my bike was in the back. Your bike was easy to get out. So I took it.

---

**Andy:** You took my bike? My brand new bike! What happened to it?

**Robin:** Mom! Mom! Andy's going to kill me! You said you wouldn't get mad.

**Andy:** What did you do with my bike?

**Robin:** I didn't do anything. The wind did!

**Andy:** What's that supposed to mean?

**Robin:** The wind blew your bike over and the brakes broke.

*[Andy gets very angry and starts coming toward Robin.]*

**Robin:** Mom! Mom! Help!

**Mom:** What's going on here?

**Andy:** That little brat ruined my bike!

**Robin:** Mom, it was an accident. The wind blew it over.

**Mom:** It sounds like we are missing something here. A part of the story is missing.

**Andy:** Don't tell me something else is wrong with my bike. Let me at Robin!

**Mom:** No, no. Settle down. What I mean is that Robin did something wrong. Now, she owes you something, Andy.

**Robin:** But I told you, the wind did it! I don't think I owe him anything. I didn't do anything wrong.

**Andy:** You didn't do anything wrong? Why is my bike broken then?

**Mom:** Kids, kids, calm down. You still owe your brother something.

**Robin:** All right. All right. I'll get the bike repaired and pay for the repairs with my allowance.

**Mom:** That's better, but it's still not enough.

**Robin:** What more do you want from me?

---

**Mom:** You owe Andy an apology. You shouldn't have taken his bike in the first place!

**Robin:** An apology! That does it! He's always blaming me and I have to apologize. Well, I'm not going to.

**Mom:** Then you are restricted to your room until you do.

**Robin:** Mom!

**Mom:** To your room!

*[Andy shakes his head and walks away. Robin goes upstairs. Mom goes to the kitchen.]*

# Skill 25 Stating an Opinion

**Definition of Skill:** Stating a belief based upon trust or faith rather than on proven facts

**Skill Activities/ Discussions:**

1. Stress that an opinion is a person's belief. Other people may have different beliefs. Discuss what a *belief* is. Have students share beliefs they have that are not shared by other people.

2. Provide students with a list of facts and opinions from social situations (e.g., "I don't care for that hair style," "The drug store is closing down"). The students should identify which are facts and which are opinions.

3. Discuss how stating an opinion relates to such phrases as "everybody is doing it" and "all my friends think...." Have students think of other phrases people use to make their opinions appear more valid. Opinions should be stated as "I" statements. For example, I think . . , I feel . . , and I believe . . .

**Situations:**

**Home**

Your family is talking about television stars. State an opinion about your favorite star.

**School**

Your social studies class just finished a unit on South America. Your teacher is giving the class a choice between taking a test or doing a report. State your opinion on what you would rather do.

**Community**

You work in a restaurant. A customer asks you what would be good to order for lunch. State an opinion about a lunch item.

| | |
|---|---|
| **Number of Characters:** | 4 |
| **Character Description:** | Kim—A friend |
| | Ronnie—A friend |
| | Carli—A friend |
| | Austin—A friend |
| **Scene Description:** | Four friends are trying to decide what they want to do for the weekend. They all give their opinions about some activities. |

**Kim:** Hi, everybody! It's Friday! Isn't it great? No school for two days!

**Ronnie:** What should we do this weekend?

**Carli:** There's a new Tom Cruise movie playing downtown. I think he is so good-looking!

**Austin:** He is good-looking, all right. The weather is supposed to be nice. Why don't we do something outside? I think hiking in to the falls and having a picnic would be fun.

**Kim:** That sounds like a good idea to me. We could start early and spend the day.

**Carli:** How early do you want to start? I have a dental appointment at 10:00.

**Ronnie:** It would be pretty hard to go to the falls after 10:00.

**Austin:** Why don't we go go-carting? There's a special coupon in the paper for a discount on four or more tickets. I really think go-carting is a lot of fun. If it's hot when we are finished, we can go swimming at the pool.

**Kim:** We could still have a picnic in the park afterwards.

**Carli:** That's fine with me. I like picnics, go-carting, and swimming.

**Ronnie:** That's OK with me, too! When should we meet?

*[The four friends continue discussing their weekend plans.]*

## Script **B** Stating an Opinion

| | |
|---|---|
| **Number of Characters:** | 3 |
| **Character Description:** | April—A friend |
| | Chris—A friend |
| | Kyle—A friend |
| **Scene Description:** | Three friends are shopping for clothes. |

**April:** I don't know about you, but I wouldn't be caught dead wearing a pair of blue, purple, pink, and green shorts!

**Kyle:** I like 'em.

**April:** That just goes to show what you think. Don't you know that most people prefer solid colors? That's why there are so many of these shorts left! They aren't solid colors!

**Kyle:** Hey, wait a minute! I'm a person and I don't always like solid colors. How do you know that "most people" like solid colors better?

**April:** Oh, I just heard it somewhere.

**Chris:** Are you sure it's not just your opinion?

*[April goes over to the sweaters. She quickly changes the subject.]*

**April:** I really like these shaker sweaters. What do you think?

**Chris:** They're OK, but most people look so fat wearing them.

**Kyle:** Here we go again with another opinion. I wish you two would learn that it's OK to have an opinion. But it makes me mad when people say "most people this" and "everybody says that." Unless you are out conducting surveys with a lot of people, I don't think you should say things about what a lot of people think. We really don't know, and that's my opinion!

**Chris:** Well, I was telling you what I thought.

**Kyle:** Fine. Tell me. Don't try to make me believe that everybody in this world agrees with you.

**April:** Boy, Kyle. You're sure getting hyper!

**Kyle:** Yeah, I guess I am. Come on, let's go get something to eat.

*[The three walk together to a restaurant.]*

# Skill 26 — Agreeing/Disagreeing

| | |
|---|---|
| **Definition of Skill:** | • Holding the same opinion as another person (agreeing) |
| | • Holding a different opinion from another person (disagreeing) |

**Skill Activities/ Discussions:**

1. Discuss the idea that no two people agree on everything and that it is all right to express their disagreement, as long as it is expressed in the right way.

2. List subjects on which teens and parents typically disagree, and talk about why they have different perspectives.

3. Discuss what could happen if people pretend to agree with someone, when they really disagree.

4. Talk about what it means to be in a *disagreeable* mood or in an *agreeable* mood.

**Situations:**

**Home**
Your parents think you should not be involved in any after-school activities so you can devote all your time to studying. Demonstrate how you would disagree with them.

**School**
Your teacher gives you two days to complete a big homework assignment. Everyone in class, including you, thinks that will not be enough time. Show how you could express your disagreement.

**Community**
You are shopping for your dad's birthday. The salesclerk suggests that you buy him a shirt. Demonstrate how you would agree.

| | |
|---|---|
| **Number of Characters:** | 3 |
| **Character Description:** | Ketisha—A friend |
| | Linda—A friend |
| | Wendy—A friend |
| **Scene Description:** | The scene begins while Ketisha, Linda, and Wendy are talking to each other in Linda's basement. |

**Ketisha:** Hey, did you two get a chance to meet the new kid at school yet?

**Linda:** Do you mean that guy in Mr. Peterson's class?

**Ketisha:** Yeah, I think his name is Dave.

**Linda:** You mean the one who says he's a football player? Another "no mind." All we need at this school is another dumb jock.

**Wendy:** I remember having a discussion about this once before with you. And as I recall, we even ended up having a fight about it.

**Linda:** I remember, too. But you've got to admit, they usually can't do anything but throw a ball.

**Wendy:** Linda, you know I like you, and you're my friend, but I have to disagree with your feelings about people in sports. What you're doing is stereo-typing Dave and making a judgment about him before you even get to know him.

**Ketisha:** I agree with you, Wendy. My cousin is on the golf and basketball teams and he is close to being a 4.0 student. Besides that, Linda, you're a good person and you happen to have blonde hair. Do you want people stereo-typing you as an airhead?

**Linda:** Come on, you two, give me a break! I guess I just said that about Dave without really thinking.

**Ketisha:**  How about it if we introduce you to him on Monday?

**Linda:**  OK, then I'll ask him what his grade point is.

*[The girls start laughing and no one's feelings are hurt.]*

| | |
|---|---|
| **Number of Characters:** | 3 |
| **Character Description:** | Frank—A friend |
| | Luke—A friend |
| | Shoo—A friend |
| **Scene Description:** | The scene begins with all three friends walking home from school together. |

**Frank:** I'm glad it's finally Friday. What a week! I had three big tests!

**Luke:** What do you guys want to do this weekend?

**Shoo:** Let's go to the mall! They still have that car exhibit.

**Frank:** Bad idea! We went there last weekend. Let's think of something different.

*[All three of them think as they walk down the street.]*

**Luke:** Hey, I've got an idea! Why don't we rent a canoe and go down the river?

**Shoo:** Yeah! We could work on our tans. I hear the water is up pretty high.

**Frank:** You two have to be crazy. I bet it costs too much and it sounds like a lot of hard work. Come on. Think of something better.

**Shoo:** We could take our bikes to the river and fish.

**Frank:** Don't be stupid! Everyone knows there aren't any fish there!

*[Shoo and Luke start getting irritated at the way Frank is disagreeing with their ideas.]*

**Luke:** Well, if it's windy, we could get one of those triple decker kites.

**Shoo:** What is a triple decker kite?

**Luke:** It's like three kites all hooked to each other. It looks really cool when it's up.

**Frank:** Forget it. You wouldn't catch me flying a kite. What if somebody sees us?

**Luke:** You think all our ideas are so stupid, but I haven't heard you come up with any yet.

**Frank:** That's because none of your ideas have been any good.

**Shoo:** Look, Frank, I don't mind if you disagree with us, but I do mind it when you tell me I'm stupid and that my ideas are dumb. If we're that stupid, then why don't you just do you own thing this weekend?

**Frank:** Fine!

*[Shoo and Luke walk away feeling upset*
*with how Frank treated them.]*

# Skill 27     Convincing Others

**Definition of Skill:**    Causing a person to believe as the speaker does

**Skill Activities/ Discussions:**

1. List times when convincing one or more people may be necessary (e.g., during a job interview, when asking for more allowance).

2. Engage in a role play in which a pushy salesperson is attempting to sell a stereo. Ask the students to identify what is wrong in the situation. Discuss how the salesperson can be convincing without being pushy.

3. Discuss the difference between *pressuring* a person into doing an activity and *convincing* a person.

**Situations:**

**Home**

You want to borrow your brother's (sister's) new sweater. Convince him (her) to loan it to you.

**School**

You are in math class. Your teacher announces that a test will be given tomorrow on fractions. Convince your teacher to postpone the test until the class has had more practice.

**Community**

You are selling magazines for school. The money will be used to purchase new software for the computers. Convince a neighbor to buy a subscription.

| Number of Characters: | 2 |
|---|---|
| Character Description: | Del—A high school student |
| | Ms. Jones—Personnel director for the city pools |
| Scene Description: | Del is in an interview with Ms. Jones for a lifeguard position. |

**Ms. Jones:** I'm very pleased to meet you, Del. Your swim coach recommends you highly.

**Del:** Thank you. I've been looking forward to this interview.

**Ms. Jones:** Why don't you tell me about yourself? Try to include as much of your swimming background as you can in your description.

**Del:** Well, I've been swimming since I was two or three years old. I started swimming for the city team when I was in grade school and am still on the team. I've learned a lot about competition. Now that I'm older, I help train the younger kids.

**Ms. Jones:** Tell me a little bit about your schooling.

**Del:** I'll be a junior next year. I like school most of the time and have almost a "B" average. The reason I want this job is because I would like to start saving money for college.

**Ms. Jones:** Very impressive! I must tell you that I have 10 interviews and only two jobs. Try to convince me to hire you for one of the jobs.

**Del:** I think my skills speak for themselves. I am, of course, a certified life-saver. Beyond my swimming skills, I am dependable and responsible. I think the references I have you will tell you that. Without bragging, I enjoy people and I get along with all ages.

**Ms. Jones:** Very convincing, Del. In all fairness, I need to finish interviewing. I can tell you that you have an excellent chance of being hired. I'll let you know tomorrow.

**Del:** Thanks. I'd appreciate that.

*[Del gets up to leave.]*

## Script B     Convincing Others

| | |
|---|---|
| **Number of Characters:** | 3 |
| **Character Description:** | George—A shoe salesperson |
| | Hillary—A teenager |
| | Mrs. Stone—Hillary's mother |
| **Scene Description:** | Mrs. Stone and Hillary are shopping for shoes. |

**George:** Hello, ladies! What can I do for you today?

**Mrs. Stone:** My daughter is looking for a pair of navy blue dress shoes.

**George:** Yes, we have just what you want. In fact, we have a number of shoes on sale which you may be interested in. What size do you wear, miss?

**Hillary:** I usually wear a 7½.

**George:** Did you say 7½? That's perfect. We have a wide selection of shoes in that size. You may decide to buy more than one pair!

*[George leaves and comes back with an armful of shoe boxes.]*

**George:** Here we are, ladies! Try these on for size!

**Hillary:** But these aren't navy blue!

**George:** No problem. They're neutral. They will go with any color. Try them!

**Mrs. Stone:** But Hillary wants navy blue!

**George:** Of course. Just let her try these. I'll guarantee she'll love them!

*[Hillary reluctantly tries the shoes on.]*

**George:** Well?

**Hillary:** They are comfortable, but . . .

**George:** Get up and walk in them. Get the feel of the rich leather uppers. Aren't they wonderful? They usually sell for $45, but for you ladies, you can have them for $40. What do you say?

**Hillary:** Forty dollars? But I wanted blue!

**George:** I'll bring you blue. Just say that you'll take these. What do you say, little mother?

**Mrs. Stone:** Young man, I've had it with your pushiness! You won't sell us those shoes, or any shoes, because we're leaving!

# Skill 28     Giving Information

**Definition of Skill:** Providing knowledge or facts in an organized manner within a specific situation

**Skill Activities/ Discussions:**

1. Present a situation in which information is given in a disorganized manner. Ask the students in what way they would change how the information was given to make it more organized.

2. Have selected students give directions to well-known places in the community. Have the rest of the class guess where the places are.

3. Discuss the terms *relevant* and *irrelevant*. Apply these terms to giving information.

**Situations:**

**Home**
Class rings are now available for your class. To convince your parents to buy you one, give them information about the ring.

**School**
The principal has asked you to show a new student around the school. Give the student information about the cafeteria.

**Community**
You work as a clerk in a store. Give a customer information on where to find the radios in the store.

| Number of Characters: | 3 |
|---|---|
| Character Description: | Lisa—A friend |
| | Andrea—A friend |
| | Josh—A friend |
| Scene Description: | Lisa, Andrea, and Josh are walking home from school. They are discussing an upcoming dance. |

**Lisa:** This dance is supposed to be great! We'll be having a band and everything!

**Andrea:** The band is great! I heard them play last summer.

**Josh:** Who's playing?

**Andrea:** Woodland.

**Josh:** Woodland! Are you kidding? They are great! I might even go to this dance!

**Lisa:** You mean you are actually going to take time off from basketball to go to a dance?

**Josh:** A guy as to have some fun once in a while.

**Andrea:** It's about time. Sometimes I think that basketball is glued to your head!

**Josh:** If I decide to go, how do I get a ticket?

**Lisa:** You can get tickets two ways. You can buy them ahead of time or you can buy them at the door.

**Andrea:** It will really pay to buy these tickets ahead of time. If you do, the tickets will cost $3. If you buy them at the door, they will cost $5.

**Lisa:** Tickets go on sale on Monday. The dance is on Friday night from 7 to 11.

**Andrea:** Josh, do you think you can put down your basketball long enough to come?

**Josh:** Who says I'm going to put down my ball? I'm going to bring it along and dribble to the music. Thanks for giving me the information, though.

**Lisa:** Ha, ha!

*[The three continue walking and talking.]*

## Script B — Giving Information

| Number of Characters: | 5 |
|---|---|
| Character Description: | Mr. Bill Peters—Father of Marv and Gwendy |
| | Mrs. Peters—Mother of Marv and Gwendy |
| | Marv—A teenager |
| | Gwendy—A teenager |
| | Sam McDonald—A volunteer at the information center |
| Scene Description: | The Peters family is on vacation. They stop at an information center in a small town. They would like information about the local restaurants. |

**Marv:** I hope there is a restaurant close by. I'm starved!

**Gwendy:** Me, too! I could eat about five thick, juicy burgers!

**Mrs. Peters:** Bill, there's an information booth. Let's stop and ask about the local restaurants.

**Mr. Peters:** That's a good idea!

*[Mr. Peters parks the car and goes into the information center.]*

**Mr. Peters:** Hi, I'm Bill Peters. We're just passing through. I was wondering if you could recommend a good restaurant.

**Sam:** Howdy, I'm Sam McDonald. You're just passing through, huh? Where did you come from?

**Mr. Peters:** We drove from California.

**Sam:** I'll bet California is a lot different from these parts!

**Mr. Peters:** I have a hungry family waiting, Mr. McDonald. Could you give me information about a good restaurant?

**Sam:** I can't do that.

| | |
|---|---|
| **Mr. Peters:** | Why? |
| **Sam:** | I can't tell you one's better than another. It's bad for business. I just tell people they're all good! |
| **Mr. Peters:** | Well, where is a restaurant then? |
| **Sam:** | Which restaurant? We have seven. |
| **Mr. Peters:** | *[Impatiently]* Any restaurant! You pick one! |
| **Sam:** | I can't. |
| **Mr. Peters:** | Why not? |
| **Sam:** | I already told you. It's bad for business. Here's a phone book. Look up "Restaurants." I'll tell you about each one. |
| **Mr. Peters:** | Now, we are getting somewhere! |

*[Mr. Peters flips through the pages until he finds the restaurant section.]*

| | |
|---|---|
| **Mr. Peters:** | How about the Coffee Cup? |
| **Sam:** | Do you like soup and sandwiches? |
| **Mr. Peters:** | Right now, we'd like anything! |
| **Sam:** | Well, the Coffee Cup has soup and sandwiches. |
| **Mr. Peters:** | How do I find this place? |
| **Sam:** | Go down two blocks, no, maybe three blocks, and turn left. |
| **Mr. Peters:** | What's the name of the street I turn on? |
| **Sam:** | I don't know. Maybe you can stop and ask at a gas station. |
| **Mr. Peters:** | I thought I was supposed to ask you? |
| **Sam:** | You can always ask. I might not know the answer to your question, though. |
| **Mr. Peters:** | *[Sarcastically]* Thanks for your help. |

*[Mr. Peters goes back to the car.]*

**Mrs. Peters:**   Where are we going to eat?

**Mr. Peters:**   I don't know.

**Gwendy:**   Doesn't this town have restaurants?

**Mr. Peters:**   All I know is that this town has seven restaurants and one, the Coffee Cup, is located a few blocks from here.

**Marv:**   That guy sure didn't give you much information!

**Mr. Peters:**   He sure didn't.

*[The family drives off.]*

| Skill | | Dealing with Contradictions |

**Definition of Skill:**  Handling messages that are unclear and opposite of each other

**Skill Activities/ Discussions:**

1.  Act out a variety of situations in which you give an oral message, but your body language gives another message. Have the students discuss these mixed messages.

2.  Introduce such terms as *mixed messages*, *contradictions*, and *body language*. Apply these terms to the skill of *dealing with contradictions* through discussion.

3.  Discuss situations in which two oral statements are contradictory (e.g., two different directions are given for the same activity). Have students explain how they can handle these situations (e.g., ask questions, indicate that the comments were confusing).

**Situations:**  **Home**

You just received free tickets to a major league game. You asked your older sister if she would go with you. She said yes, but her body language showed that she really didn't care to go. Demonstrate how you would deal with the contradiction.

**School**

You are helping a friend with his geometry. You've explained the whole assignment. He said he understood it, but his body language told you he really didn't. Tell how you would deal with the contradiction.

**Community**

You are looking for the house where you will be baby-sitting. You stop two people and ask them for directions. Each person gives you directions and the directions are contradictory. Demonstrate dealing with the contradiction.

| | |
|---|---|
| **Number of Characters:** | 3 |
| **Character Description:** | Susan—A teenager |
| | Pam—Susan's friend |
| | Mrs. Woke—Susan's mom |
| **Scene Description:** | Susan and Pam are on a walk. Susan invites her friend, Pam, to go with her to hear a famous symphony play. |

**Susan:** My parents and I are going to hear the Gregory Symphony on Saturday. Would you like to come with us?

**Pam:** The Gregory Symphony? What do they play?

**Susan:** Usually they play all classical music—Beethoven, Bach, music like that. But on Saturday, they will be playing a pop concert.

**Pam:** *[Trying to sound interested, when she really isn't]* Gee, Susan, that sounds like fun. I guess I'll go.

**Susan:** Are you sure you want to go? You don't sound too interested.

**Pam:** Oh, sure I want to go. It will be a good experience.

**Susan:** Here's my house. I'll see you after dinner.

**Pam:** OK. See you later.

*[Susan enters her house.]*

**Susan:** Hi, Mom. What's for dinner?

**Mrs. Woke:** We're having spaghetti.

**Susan:** Sounds good. Mom, I just invited Pam to go with us on Saturday.

**Mrs. Woke:** Good. I'm glad that we will be able to use the extra ticket.

**Susan:** I want her to go, too, but I'm not sure she wants to.

**Mrs. Woke:** How's that?

| | |
|---|---|
| **Susan:** | Well, she said she wanted to go, but her expression sort of told me that she didn't want to go. |
| **Mrs. Woke:** | Did you ask her about her expression? |
| **Susan:** | I tried, but I just feel so dumb doing it. |
| **Mrs. Woke:** | It's hard to talk about feelings. But at least you'll know what Pam is thinking. |
| **Susan:** | OK. I'll talk to her. |

*[Later that evening . . .]*

| | |
|---|---|
| **Susan:** | Pam, about the concert. |
| **Pam:** | What about it? |
| **Susan:** | I sort of noticed that you really didn't seem very interested in going. |
| **Pam:** | I want to go, but . . . |
| **Susan:** | But what? |
| **Pam:** | Are you sure I won't hurt your feelings? |
| **Susan:** | I'm sure. |
| **Pam:** | I've never really listened to that kind of music much before. I'm not sure if I'll like it. |
| **Susan:** | Is that all? I thought you were mad about something. |
| **Pam:** | No. I just wasn't sure about the music. |
| **Susan:** | I felt the same way when I first went. But the musicians are so good that you'll soon forget all of your shy feelings about going. |
| **Pam:** | I feel better about going. I'm glad we talked. |
| **Susan:** | Me, too! |

| | |
|---|---|
| **Number of Characters:** | 4 |
| **Character Description:** | Shane—A delivery person |
| | Stewart—Shane's friend at work |
| | Ms. Strong—Shane's supervisor |
| | Mr. Jenkins—The manager of Shane's department |
| **Scene Description:** | Shane gets very confused when he is given contradictory instructions from his two bosses. |

**Shane:** They did it to me again!

**Stewart:** Who's they and what did they do?

**Shane:** Ms. Strong and Mr. Jenkins are always giving me opposite directions. One tells me to fold. One tells me to unfold. I get so darn confused!

**Stewart:** Why don't you just tell them that they are contradicting each other?

**Shane:** What? You want me to tell two bosses that they have made a mistake? Who knows what might happen! I may get fired! I'll just go on being confused, I guess.

**Stewart:** Here comes Ms. Strong.

**Shane:** She's probably going to give me more instructions.

**Stewart:** I'd better get back to unloading this delivery.

**Shane:** OK, see you around.

*[Ms. Strong approaches Shane.]*

**Ms. Strong:** There you are. I see you are packing the paper for the Fuller project. Good. I'd like to get that shipment out as soon as possible.

**Shane:** Yes, Ms. Strong. I'll try to hurry.

**Ms. Strong:** Check with me before you leave. I'd like to know how far you got.

| | |
|---|---|
| **Shane:** | I'll be glad to do that. |

*[Ms. Strong leaves. A little later Mr. Jenkins approaches.]*

| | |
|---|---|
| **Mr. Jenkins:** | Shane, what are you working on? I thought I told you to get the Butler shipment finished? |
| **Shane:** | I know, sir, but Ms. Strong told me to . . . |
| **Mr. Jenkins:** | I think you had better work on the Butler shipment and put this one aside. |
| **Shane:** | Yes, sir. |

*[At the end of the day . . .]*

| | |
|---|---|
| **Ms. Strong:** | Well, Shane, how did you do? |
| **Shane:** | Oh, I did quite well with the Butler shipment. |
| **Ms. Strong:** | The Butler shipment! What were you doing that for? |
| **Shane:** | Mr. Jenkins told me to . . . |
| **Ms. Strong:** | From now on, Shane, work on one job and get it done. If you try to do too much, nothing gets finished! |
| **Shane:** | Yes, Ms. Strong. Good night. |

## Skill 30 — Starting a Friendship

**Definition of Skill:** Developing a liking for another person based upon common interests

**Skill Activities/ Discussions:**

1. Brainstorm a list of places where friends can be made. Use the lists to help the students arrive at the generalization that friends can be made almost anywhere.

2. Discuss the phrase *common interests*. Have students tell about their friends and their common interests.

3. Have students describe their ideal friend. Contrast this with a description of someone with whom they would not want to start a friendship.

**Situations:**

**Home**

Your sister brings a friend home from school. Even though she is younger than you, you find her interesting. Show how you would get to know her better.

**School**

A new student has been assigned a locker next to yours. Demonstrate how you would get to know that student better.

**Community**

You sit next to a person on the city bus. Begin a conversation and discover your common interests.

| Number of Characters: | 3 |
|---|---|
| **Character Description:** | Mrs. Jacob—An eighty-year-old woman |
| | Jason—Mrs. Jacob's friend |
| | George—Jason's friend |
| **Scene Description:** | Jason is talking to his friend, George, outside of Mrs. Jacob's house. |

**George:** Hi, Jason! Where are you going?

**Jason:** I'm going to visit Mrs. Jacob.

**George:** What do you want to visit an 80-year-old woman for?

**Jason:** I know Mrs. Jacob is old, George, but she is also my friend. She is very interesting to talk to. I love to hear the stories she tells. Did you know that she was a reporter for the Chicago Tribune, when Al Capone and the other gangsters were in Chicago?

**George:** Really?

**Jason:** Yeah! Why don't you come with me? I'll introduce you.

**George:** OK. But what do you say to an old lady? Can she even hear? Do I have to yell?

**Jason:** Don't worry. I think you will be surprised.

*[Jason knocks on the door and Mrs. Jacob answers it.]*

**Jason:** Hi, Mrs. Jacob!

**Mrs. Jacob:** Hi, Jason! I see you've brought a friend! Come in.

**Jason:** Mrs. Jacob, I'd like you to meet my friend, George. George, this is my friend, Mrs. Jacob.

**George:** Hi!

*[The boys enter the house. George looks around.]*

**George:** Wow! Do you ever have a picture collection of baseball stars! Look at this autographed picture of Joe DiMaggio. And here's one of Jackie Robinson? Is this Lou Gehrig?

**Mrs. Jacob:** Do you like baseball?

**George:** You bet! I love reading about the old baseball stars! How did you get all of these pictures?

**Mrs. Jacob:** I worked as a news reporter. Back then, women just weren't sportswriters, but that's where I started. The paper never told the readers I was a woman. My stories were always published as M. Jacob. I suppose the readers thought M. stood for Mike or Milt. They would have been surprised if they knew M. stood for Mary!

**Jason:** Mrs. Jacob, could we look at your scrapbook?

*[George gives a "bored" look, which only Jason sees.]*

**Mrs. Jacob:** Sure, Jason. I'll get it.

**Jason:** Thanks, Mrs. Jacob.

*[Jason lays the scrapbook on the table and opens the front cover.]*

**George:** Look at that! That's Al Capone! Look at the gun that Dillinger has! Who is this guy with the machine gun?

**Mrs. Jacob:** That's Machine Gun Kelly. He isn't as well known as the others, but he sure killed a lot of people with that gun.

**Jason:** How have you been, Mrs. Jacob?

**Mrs. Jacob:** I've been fine. I'm always busy. I've started a new tank of fish.

**George:** Fish? Do you have fish too? I love saltwater fish! They sure are hard to raise, though.

**Mrs. Jacob:** Why don't you come into my aquarium room, George?

---

**George:** Wow! You must have 15 tanks in here!

**Mrs. Jacob:** I've had fish for most of my life, George. I keep adding tanks. Why don't you tell me a bit about your tank? Maybe we can share ideas. I agree with you that saltwater fish are very hard to raise.

*[After talking for almost an hour . . .]*

**Jason:** Well, Mrs. Jacob, I have to get my papers delivered. I'll stop by again soon.

**Mrs. Jacob:** OK, Jason.

**George:** Mrs. Jacob, do you think I could stop over again, too?

**Mrs. Jacob:** Sure, George. I'd love to talk with you again. I appreciate the ideas you gave me about the clown fish.

**George:** Thanks.

*[Jason and George say good-bye to Mrs. Jacob as they walk out the door.]*

| | |
|---|---|
| **Number of Characters:** | 3 |
| **Character Description:** | Sue—A new girl in the neighborhood |
| | Jeremy—A teenage baseball player |
| | Isaac—Jeremy's teammate |
| **Scene Description:** | Jeremy's baseball team is practicing in the park. Sue is watching the game. A foul ball lands in the area where Sue is sitting. She gets up to find the ball and runs into Jeremy. |

**Sue:** I'll get the ball.

**Jeremy:** Thanks a lot.

**Sue:** *[Holding the ball]* Hi, my name is Sue. What's yours?

**Jeremy:** I'm Jeremy.

**Isaac:** Hey, Jeremy! Let's get playing.

**Sue:** I just moved here from Cleveland. I'll be going to Eastland.

**Jeremy:** That's nice. Can I have the ball?

**Sue:** Oh, you don't need this ball yet. Why don't you take a break and talk to me? I don't know anyone yet, but you.

**Jeremy:** I've got to get back to the game. Give me the ball.

**Isaac:** What's the holdup, Jeremy? Let's get playing.

**Jeremy:** I'm trying to get our ball back.

**Sue:** Where do you live, Jeremy?

**Jeremy:** Listen, Sue. I know you want to make friends, but now is not the time. Maybe some other time, when I'm not busy. Now, give me the ball.

**Sue:** OK, here's your ball.

*[Sue throws the ball on the ground and walks away.*
*Jeremy picks it up and goes back to the game.]*

**Isaac:** Who was that girl, anyway?

**Jeremy:** Somebody new. She wants to make friends.

**Isaac:** She'd better find a better way or else she'll be making a lot of enemies!

**Jeremy:** That's for sure. Let's get back to the game.

| Skill | **31** | Giving Emotional Support |

**Definition of Skill:** Providing encouragement to someone who is making a difficult decision, is having difficulty doing a specific activity, or is feeling depressed

**Skill Activities/ Discussions:**

1. Discuss examples of times when friends need to support each other (e.g., a death in the family, a poor grade).

2. Provide situations in which one person needs to support another. Discuss appropriate topics of conversation for those times.

3. Make a list of statements that would be supportive to another individual. The list may include: "I know exactly how you are feeling," "I see that you are feeling _____," "Is there anything I can do?"

**Situations:**

**Home**
Your friend had a dog for 12 years and it just died. Your friend is feeling very sad. Demonstrate how you would provide emotional support.

**School**
Your friend has to give a speech. She is afraid to get up in front of the class. Encourage her to do so.

**Community**
A little child is lost in a large department store. Demonstrate how you would help to support and comfort the child.

| | |
|---|---|
| **Number of Characters:** | 3 |
| **Character Description:** | Jeff—A teenager |
| | Joel—Jeff's friend |
| | Linda—Jeff's friend |
| **Scene Description:** | Jeff has been selected as a finalist in the chess competition. He is extremely nervous and must do better than he has ever done to win. His friends, Joel and Linda, are giving support and encouragement. The scene takes place at school. Joel and Linda are walking up to Jeff. |

**Joel:** Congrats, Jeff! I knew you could do it! You just outsmarted that other guy you were playing against.

**Jeff:** Thanks, Joel! The win was easier than I had expected. It's the finals I'm worried about now! I'm going to be playing the best from ten schools!

**Linda:** The competition is stiff all right! But just look at all of the competition you've had already.

**Joel:** That's right, Jeff! The game is the same. The rules are the same. You will just have different partners.

**Linda:** When you think about it, nothing has changed. You may even be playing people you've already played.

**Jeff:** I guess when you think about the tournament in those terms, the situation doesn't sound too bad after all! Thanks for the support!

---

| | |
|---|---|
| **Number of Characters:** | 3 |
| **Character Description:** | George Stull—Heather's father |
| | Heather—A teenager |
| | Emily—Heather's friend |
| **Scene Description:** | The scene takes place when Heather takes her "behind the wheel" driver's test. |

**Heather:** I am so nervous, Dad. I hope that I pass the test.

**George:** You will, honey. Don't worry.

**Heather:** There's the examiner. I'd better go.

*[A half an hour later . . .]*

**George:** How did it go, Heather?

**Heather:** Don't ask!

**George:** You mean I don't have to share my car with you yet?

**Heather:** Dad, I don't want to talk about it.

*[Heather and her father arrive home.]*

**Heather:** I'm going over to Emily's.

*[At Emily's house . . .]*

**Emily:** Hi, Heather. How was your driver's test? Were you nervous?

**Heather:** Emily, I'm so embarrassed! I didn't pass the test!

**Emily:** *[Starts laughing]* You didn't pass! I've never heard anything so ridiculous! Come on, Heather, quit kidding me. Come on, let's see if your dad will let us take the car.

*[Heather starts to cry.]*

**Heather:**  Emily, I'm not kidding. I flunked! I'm a failure!

**Emily:**  I guess you are. I mean . . . I'm surprised you didn't pass.

**Heather:**  Stop, Emily. You are making me feel worse.

**Emily:**  OK, I'll stop. Are you sure you're not kidding me?

**Heather:**  *[Sounding angry]* Emily!

| Skill | | Attending and Ignoring |
|-------|---|------------------------|

**Definition of Skill:**
- Being careful to watch and listen to others (attending)
- Paying no attention to others (ignoring)

**Skill Activities/ Discussions:**

1. Teach students the following rule: "Attention pays off for both positive and negative behaviors." Discuss this rule with the students. Define such terms as *attention*, *positive behavior*, and *negative behavior*.

2. Play "Attention Getter." Send one student out in the hall. Give the student in the hall a list of behaviors such as clapping, whistling, foot tapping, singing, etc. Include pencil tapping on the list. Tell the student to try to get the attention of the class for at least 30 seconds by acting out each behavior on the list. Tell the other students to pay attention to the student in the hall only when tapping a pencil. The students can tell the pencil tapper they "like the beat." They can smile or frown. They can make any gesture or verbal comment which attends to the pencil tapper. Stress that the class should attend only to the pencil tapping. After this experiment, discuss the results. Have the student in the hall tell which actions drew the most attention.

3. Once the students understand how attention increases behavior, ask them how certain behaviors can be decreased. Introduce the concept of ignoring, by presenting two situations. In one, a person ignores the negative behavior of another and that person stops the negative behavior. In the second situation, the negative behavior is attended to. As a result, the behavior gets worse.

**Situations:**

**Home**
Your sister is 13 and still talks baby talk. You family decides to pay attention and talk to her when she talks in a regular voice. Ignore her when she talks baby talk.

### School

You have a friend who talks very loudly. You and your friends decide to ignore him when he speaks loudly. Talk to him when he speaks in a normal tone of voice.

### Community

It's late at night. The show you attended with a friend has just ended. As you leave, a stranger begins talking to you. You and your friend ignore him, hoping that he will go away. Demonstrate how you would give the stranger no attention.

| | |
|---|---|
| **Number of Characters:** | 5 |
| **Character Description:** | Duane—A teenager |
| | Mr. Berg—Duane's father |
| | Kim—A friend |
| | Duke—A friend |
| | Renee—A friend |
| **Scene Description:** | The scene takes place in Duane's home. He is leaving his room wearing a new pair of pants, a new sweater, and a new shirt. Duane's father sees him leaving. |

**Mr. Berg:** Duane, is that you? You look great, son! Is this a special occasion?

**Duane:** No, Dad. I just got tired of my holey jeans.

**Mr. Berg:** You sure are going to have the girls following you!

**Duane:** That sure would be nice, Dad!

*[Duane walks to school and is at his locker.]*

**Renee:** Duane! You look super!

**Duane:** Thanks, Renee. I needed a change!

**Renee:** I sure like the change.

*[Kim and Duke walk up.]*

**Kim:** Duane! What did you do to yourself? I mean, clean pants and a new sweater! Are you sick or something?

**Duke:** You look great! Now, maybe I can invite you over to my house without my parents thinking you're a dirt ball.

*[All day long Duane receives compliments on his appearance.*
*After school, he hurries home to clean out his closet.]*

**Mr. Berg:** What are you doing, Duane?

**Duane:** I'm throwing out these old clothes. I kind of like getting dressed up!

**Mr. Berg:** I see.

**Duane:** You were right, Dad! Girls followed me around all day. Their attention was great!

*[The next day Duane wears another new outfit.]*

| | |
|---|---|
| **Number of Characters:** | 4 |
| **Character Description:** | Miss Aspen—A teacher |
| | Jerry—A student |
| | Carmen—A student |
| | Jody—A student |
| **Scene Description:** | The scene takes place in English class. One boy, Jerry, demands constant attention, whether it is good or bad. |

**Miss Aspen:** For tomorrow, I'd like you to finish reading the play. You can have the rest of the hour to work on your reading.

*[The class is reading quietly. Jerry nervously looks around. He taps his pencil and whistles quietly.]*

**Jerry:** *[Loudly]* Ah, Miss Aspen? Can I go to the bathroom?

**Miss Aspen:** Yes, you can, Jerry.

**Jerry:** Thanks.

*[Jerry gets up and leaves the classroom.]*

**Miss Aspen:** Class, I'd like to interrupt you a moment. Jerry is trying to get our attention again. Please try not to look at him or pay any attention to him. Just ignore him when he comes back.

**Carmen:** Miss Aspen, can I move? It's really hard to concentrate, sitting next to Jerry.

**Miss Aspen:** I'll let you move tomorrow. Would you please finish class in your current seat? OK, are there any questions about what we are going to do? If not, you can get back to your reading.

*[Jerry enters the room.]*

**Jerry:** *[Loudly]* Thanks, Miss Aspen, for letting me go. Now I should be able to concentrate.

*[Jerry sits down.]*

**Jerry:** *[Shouting]* Miss Aspen, I don't understand what happened to George in the play.

*[Miss Aspen ignores him. He turns around.]*

**Jerry:** Hey, Jody, what happened to George in the play?

*[Jody ignores him.]*

**Jerry:** *[Mumbling to himself]* Nobody's talking. I guess I'll have to read.

*[Jerry begins reading. A few minutes later the bell rings. The class is dismissed. Miss Aspen decides to compliment the class for ignoring Jerry's behavior. She makes a note to herself to talk to Jerry and to compliment him for settling down and reading.]*

## Skill 33      Responding to Teasing

**Definition of Skill:**    Handling comments that annoy or make fun of a person

**Skill Activities/ Discussions:**

1. Have students discuss the times they were teased. How did they feel?

2. Discuss the words, *attention* and *ignoring*. Talk about the effects of paying attention to or ignoring teasing.

3. Differentiate between *friendly teasing* and *mean teasing*. Have students discuss how they would respond to the different types of teasing.

**Situations:**

**Home**

Your older brother is continually teasing you. He always calls you "goat face." Demonstrate how you would respond to the teasing.

**School**

You got the only "A" on a math test. Your friends are teasing you about being teacher's pet. Show how you would respond.

**Community**

A group of boys drive by you on the sidewalk and make an obscene gesture. Show how you would respond.

| | |
|---|---|
| **Number of Characters:** | 5 |
| **Character Description:** | Shelly—A teenager |
| | Betty—A teenager |
| | Candy—A teenager |
| | Keith—A teenager |
| | Jarrod—A teenager |
| **Scene Description:** | The scene begins with Shelly, Betty, and Candy sitting in the park talking. Keith and Jarrod come by and start teasing Candy. |

**Shelly:** It sure is a nice day!

**Betty:** I love the spring. It's almost warm enough to swim!

**Candy:** Let's go walk by the water. Maybe the ducks will be swimming.

*[Keith and Jarrod are a distance behind the girls.]*

**Keith:** Isn't that Candy Phillips ahead of us?

**Jarrod:** I think it is. She is something else!

**Keith:** I can't say much for her other two friends, though.

**Jarrod:** Let's sneak up on them. I love to tease Candy!

*[As the girls are walking, they hear a bush move behind them.]*

**Jarrod:** Hey, Candy! Are you as sweet as your name is?

**Candy:** *[To her friends]* They are at it again! I hate it when they make fun of me.

**Betty:** You get so much attention from the boys. How can you hate it?

**Candy:** I wouldn't mind if they would just talk to me, but they don't. It's always teasing.

**Keith:**    Oh, Candy. Are you as sweet as sugar?

**Jarrod:**    Hey, sweetie!

**Candy:**    I just hate it!

**Shelly:**    Just keep walking. Pretend you don't hear them.

**Betty:**    If you let them know you hate their teasing, they'll just keep it up. The more you pay attention to them, the more they will tease you.

*[The girls keep walking without looking back.]*

**Jarrod:**    Candy pretended like she didn't even see us!

**Keith:**    I guess teasing her isn't going to get us her attention.

## Script B — Responding to Teasing

| | |
|---|---|
| **Number of Characters:** | 5 |
| **Character Description:** | Greg—A teenager |
| | Jason—A teenager |
| | Mark—A teenager |
| | Dan—A teenager |
| | Mr. Billings—The teacher |
| **Scene Description:** | The scene begins in the hallway at school, where Jason, Mark, and Dan are teasing Greg about his haircut. |

**Jason:** Hey, guys! There's Greg. Look at that haircut!

**Mark:** It looks like someone came at him with a hedge clipper.

**Dan:** *[To Greg]* Hey, Spike! Have you seen a barber lately?

**Greg:** Shut up, Dan!

**Jason:** What's the matter, Greg? Oh, I mean, Spike?

**Greg:** I think you forgot my name, jerk! My name is Greg!

**Mark:** Not anymore, it isn't. I think Spike is better since you got that haircut!

**Greg:** My haircut is my business, not yours.

**Dan:** If I were you, I'd wear a hat!

**Greg:** Shut up!

**Mr. Billings:** What's all the shouting about?

**Greg:** *[Looking at the others]* Nothing!

**Mr. Billings:** Well, if nothing is going on, there is no reason to stand around. You boys should head for class.

*[The boys begin to leave.]*

| | |
|---|---|
| **Mr Billings:** | Greg, I'd like to see you for a minute, please. |
| **Greg:** | Yes, Mr. Billings? |
| **Mr. Billings:** | Greg, were those boys teasing you? |
| **Greg:** | Yeah, I guess they were. |
| **Mr. Billings:** | I thought so. You sounded pretty angry. |
| **Greg:** | I guess I did. |
| **Mr. Billings:** | You know, reacting that way will only make the boys tease you more. |
| **Greg:** | I know, but it's hard to ignore them. |
| **Mr. Billings:** | Yes, but that's what you have to do. |
| **Greg:** | Isn't there anything else I can do? |
| **Mr. Billings:** | You think about it. |
| **Greg:** | I will. I'd better get to class. Bye. |

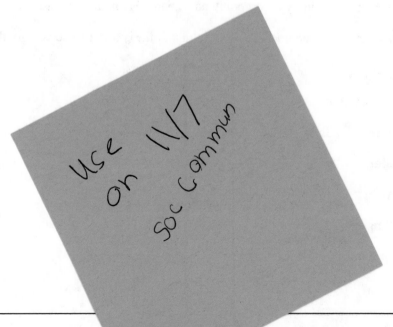

# Skill 34 — Peer Pressure

**Definition of Skill:** Being convinced to do something you do not want to do by other people in your age group

Note: Although peer pressure may have positive effects in some situations (e.g., a group of friends trying to get good grades), adolescents typically have a difficult time resisting peers who want to lead them into trouble. Therefore, emphasis will be placed upon learning to identify negative pressure and learning to say no to it.

**Skill Activities/ Discussions:**

1. Provide situations in which one or more people are pressuring another person. From these situations, have the students arrive at a definition of *peer pressure* through deductive reasoning.

2. Brainstorm a list of situations in which students receive peer pressure.

3. Have a discussion in which students suggest ways of saying no to various types of peer pressure.

4. Have students identify times when peer pressure may be beneficial.

**Situations:**

**Home**

You and your older brother are home alone. You both would like to order a pizza, but neither one of you has any money. Your brother tries to persuade you to take the money that your parents left in their bedroom. Demonstrate how you would deal with the pressure.

**School**

It's a beautiful spring day. A group of your friends are going to skip school after lunch. They try to pressure you into going with them. Show how you would resist their pressure.

**Community**

You have a paper route. You need extra money for tickets to the concert. Your friends are trying to convince you to keep the money you collected for the papers. Demonstrate how you would deal with the pressure.

| **Number of Characters:** | 4 |
|---|---|
| **Character Description:** | Quinn—A teenager |
| | Jerry—A teenager |
| | Alex—A teenager |
| | Greg—A teenager |
| **Scene Description:** | Quinn, Jerry, Alex, and Greg are sitting around a campfire one evening. |

**Quinn:** Isn't this great! Look at all those stars!

**Alex:** You know what's even better than this night?

**Greg:** No, what?

**Alex:** We don't have any school on Monday! We can have three days of fun.

**Quinn:** Speaking of fun, guys. I just happen to have something to add to our enjoyment.

**Alex:** *[Laughing]* Where are the girls, Quinn? Do you have them hiding in your sleeping bag?

**Quinn:** No girls, Alex. Just these.

*[Quinn holds out three bottles of wine.]*

**Jerry:** Wine! Great! I love it.

**Quinn:** Remember last spring? You loved it so much you were sick for three hours. Yuck! Don't remind me.

**Greg:** *[Lifting a bottle to his lips]* Well, guys, cheers!

*[The boys pass the bottle and all take a drink except Alex.]*

**Quinn:** Hey, look at the party pooper. What's wrong with you, Alex? Are you sick or something?

**Greg:** Here, Alex. Take a drink. If you're sick, this will make you feel better.

**Jerry:** Alex, what are you afraid of? We are in the middle of the woods.

**Quinn:** It's only us and the mosquitoes. Come on, Alex.

**Alex:** Listen, guys. We have been friends for a long time. Cut the pressure. If you guys want to drink, fine. But quit bugging me!

**Quinn:** Okay, Alex. Just don't go crazy on us!

*[The boys continue talking.]*

**Number of Characters:**   5

**Character Description:**   Rolanda—A teenager

José—A teenager

Victor—A teenager

Mr. Calmo—Rolanda's father

Mrs. Calmo—Rolanda's mother

**Scene Description:**   Victor and José are visiting Rolanda at her house. Rolanda is home alone.

**Victor:**   Rolanda, what are we going to do?

**Rolanda:**   Why don't we watch some movies? My parents just rented three new videos.

**José:**   Sounds good to me! I'll get them set up.

**Rolanda:**   I'll make some popcorn.

**Victor:**   I'll help.

*[Victor and Rolanda go into the kitchen.*
*Victor sees some keys on the table.]*

**Victor:**   Rolanda, what are the keys for?

**Rolanda:**   My parents' MG.

**Victor:**   You mean that little red sports car?

**Rolanda:**   Yeah. What are you so excited about?

**Victor:**   I love those cars! I'll bet it really goes fast, too!

**Rolanda:**   I don't know how fast it goes.

**Victor:**   Let's find out! José, come in the kitchen.

---

**José:** What do you want?

**Victor:** We're in luck! Rolanda's parents left the keys to the MG home.

**José:** So?

**Victor:** So, let's go for a ride.

**Rolanda:** I don't think that's a good idea. None of us has a license yet.

**Victor:** I have been driving since I was eight. Anyway, we'd just go around the block. Come on, Rolanda!

**José:** Doesn't the MG hold only two people?

**Victor:** So what! We're skinny! We can fit. What do you say, Rolanda?

**Rolanda:** Well, OK. As long as you promise that we'll be right back.

**Victor:** I promise.

*[Victor, Rolanda, and José pile into the small car and drive off.]*

**Rolanda:** Victor, you said we would be right home. We've already driven over an hour!

**Victor:** Calm down. We're heading home now.

**José:** This was a perfect night for a ride! I had a great time.

*[The car turns the corner on Rolanda's block.]*

**Rolanda:** Hey, there's a police car in our driveway!

**Victor:** Oh, oh! It looks like Rolanda's parents are home!

*[The car pulls into the driveway and Victor, Rolanda, and José get out.]*

**Mr. Calmo:** *[Angrily]* Where have you been?

**Rolanda:** *[Quietly]* We went for a ride.

| | |
|---|---|
| **Mrs. Calmo:** | *[Angrily]* We can see that! Three underage kids driving around. How nice! |
| **Rolanda:** | What are the police here for? |
| **Mr. Calmo:** | When we came home, we found you and the car gone. We thought something had happened. |
| **Rolanda:** | I'm fine. |
| **Mrs. Calmo:** | I think you had better wait in the house. |
| **Mr. Calmo:** | Officer, thank you for coming by. Boys, you are no longer welcome here. Good night. |

*[The family goes into the house. José and Victor leave.]*

## Skill 35 — Joining In

**Definition of Skill:** Finding a way of entering into an activity or a conversation without disrupting those involved

**Skill Activities/ Discussions:**

1. Present a situation in which one person "joins in" inappropriately. Have students identify what was wrong and suggest more appropriate ways of joining in.

2. Ask students to distinguish between *joining in, interrupting,* and *butting into a conversation.*

3. List situations when joining in may be desired or necessary.

**Situations:**

**Home**
You get home from a friend's house and discover your family playing cards. You would like to join in. Show how you could do this.

**School**
A group of friends is talking in the hall. Demonstrate how you join in.

**Community**
You are at an annual picnic for the employees of a local store. There are too many people for the number of staff members cooking. Ask if you can join in and help.

| | |
|---|---|
| **Number of Characters:** | 3 |
| **Character Description:** | Todd—A teenager |
| | June—A teenager |
| | Sue—A teenager |
| **Scene Description:** | Todd and June are eating lunch in a crowded restaurant. Sue is looking for a place to sit, and the only seat left is at their table. All three are on lunch break from the same store. |

**Todd:** It sure is crowded here today!

**June:** It's always like this at lunch time. This place is really conveniently located for a lot of people from work.

**Todd:** The person who just came in looks familiar. Do you know her?

**June:** That's Sue Grant. She works in the same department I do.

**Todd:** She's coming in our direction.

**Sue:** Hi, June! Would you mind if I joined you? The place is so crowded that this is the only seat!

**June:** Sure, Sue! Have a seat! It's always pretty crowded here at noon.

**Sue:** It's the only place to eat that's close by.

*[Sue looks over at Todd.]*

**June:** Oh, excuse me. I'm sorry I didn't introduce you. Sue Grant, this is Todd Swanson. Todd works in the sports department.

**Sue:** Hi, Todd. It's nice to meet you.

**Todd:** It's nice to meet you too, Sue. How long have you been working for the store?

*[The conversation continues between June, Todd, and Sue.]*

---

| | |
|---|---|
| **Number of Characters:** | 4 |
| **Character Description:** | Ron—A teenager |
| | Patty—A teenager |
| | Lisa—A teenager |
| | Bill—A teenager |
| **Scene Description:** | Ron, Patty, and Lisa are talking, while waiting in line at the theater. |

**Ron:** This line is really long! I sure hope we can get into the movie.

**Patty:** Me, too! I heard that this movie is excellent!

**Lisa:** I heard that the scene where they are running through the jungle is really exciting.

**Patty:** Look who's coming!

**Ron:** Oh, no, it's Bill! Hurry up and turn your back. Maybe he won't see us!

**Lisa:** Oops, too late! Here he comes!

**Patty:** He's going to butt right in, I'm sure. He is so loud, he's embarrassing to be around.

**Bill:** *[Loudly]* Hi, Ron. Hi, Patty and Lisa! How's it going? I'm just going to step in line with you. It sure beats standing at the end of the line! Hey, Patty, wasn't that some test we had?

**Patty:** It sure was.

**Bill:** Boy, I can hardly wait to see this movie. It should be great! Hey, how come you guys are so quiet all of a sudden? You guys were sure nice to let me get in line here.

**Ron:** Actually, Bill, we do mind that you just came up and expected to join us.

**Bill:** I can see that I'm not wanted here!

---

**Patty:** Sorry, Bill. We were having a nice conversation and instead of waiting a second, you barged right into our group.

*[Bill walks away.]*

**Lisa:** I hate being so blunt.

**Ron:** But with Bill, you have to. He'll never get the message otherwise!

| Skill | 36 | Being Left Out |

**Definition of Skill:** Coping with being left out of an activity in which you would like to be included

**Skill Activities/ Discussions:**

1. Discuss with the students how someone feels when being left out. Have the students give examples of times they were left out and how they felt.

2. Discuss how being left out may provoke angry feelings in the person being excluded. The class may want to discuss confrontation skills. For example, after an individual has been left out, he may want to confront the situation and ask why, rather than to wonder.

3. Make a list of responses which can be made after an individual has been left out of an activity. Discuss each response.

**Situations:**

**Home**

You come home from seeing a friend and find your family is just leaving for dinner and a movie. You can't go because it would take you too long to get cleaned up. Demonstrate how you would react to being left out.

**School**

In gym class, the students are picking basketball teams. You were the last one picked. Because the teams would be uneven if you played, the teacher asked you to sit out. Show how you deal with being left out.

**Community**

You go out to eat with several friends. The waiter takes everyone's order but yours. He hurries off before you can give your order. Show your reaction to being left out.

| | |
|---|---|
| **Number of Characters:** | 4 |
| **Character Description:** | Angelica—An office employee |
| | Rick—Angelica's coworker |
| | Julie—Angelica's friend |
| | Mr. Zack—Angelica's boss |
| **Scene Description:** | Angelica arrives at work to find out that there is a meeting, which includes all employees but her. |

**Rick:** Angelica, you'd better check in quick! It's almost time for our meeting with Mr. Zack.

**Angelica:** What meeting?

**Rick:** Didn't you get a letter? I thought everybody got one.

**Angelica:** No, I didn't! Gosh, I hope I didn't do anything wrong!

*[A few minutes later everyone but Angelica leaves for the conference room. Angelica feels bad that she was left out. She worries about it all day at work. When Angelica goes home, she decides to talk to her friend, Julie, about the situation.]*

**Angelica:** Rick told me that Mr. Zack called a meeting for all employees, but I wasn't invited.

**Julie:** What was the meeting about?

**Angelica:** I don't know. I was too afraid to ask. I sure am curious, though. I guess I can find out from Rick tomorrow.

**Julie:** Don't you think you should talk to your boss?

**Angelica:** I guess so. I sure hope I'm not going to lose my job.

**Julie:** Call me tomorrow and let me know what happened.

**Angelica:** OK, I will.

*[The next day at work.]*

**Angelica:** Hi, Mr. Zack! Could I talk to you, please?

**Mr. Zack:** Sure, Angelica. Come in.

**Angelica:** I noticed you had a meeting for all the employees.

**Mr. Zack:** Yes, Angelica, I did.

**Angelica:** Was there a reason why I wasn't invited?

**Mr. Zack:** I'm sorry, Angelica. You should have been. We must have made a mistake. The whole purpose of the meeting was to discuss the company picnic.

**Angelica:** I was worried I had done something wrong.

**Mr. Zack:** No, Angelica. We are very pleased with your work.

**Angelica:** Thank you, Mr. Zack. Good-bye.

| | |
|---|---|
| **Number of Characters:** | 4 |
| **Character Description:** | Amber—A teenager |
| | Sue—A teenager |
| | Carlos—A teenager |
| | Greg—A teenager |
| **Scene Description:** | Amber, Sue, and Carlos are planning to go swimming during the time when Greg has to work. |

**Amber:** It's so hot out. I can barely move!

**Sue:** Let's go swimming.

**Carlos:** That sounds great!

**Greg:** Swimming is about the only way to feel comfortable in this heat.

**Amber:** Let's get our suits and meet at Carlos's house in an hour!

**Sue:** Good idea!

**Greg:** Wait a minute. It's not a good idea! I have to work in an hour!

**Carlos:** When do you want to go swimming?

**Greg:** How about tonight at 8:00? I'll be off work by then.

**Amber:** By 8:00, I'll feel like a fried egg!

**Sue:** Greg, I really want to go swimming soon!

**Greg:** *[Getting angry]* Fine. You go swimming. Think only about yourselves.

**Carlos:** I don't think you should expect us to sit around and boil in this heat just because you have to work. I'm for going swimming as soon as we can!

**Sue:** Me, too!

**Greg:** Some friends!

**Amber:** Hey, guys! We can go swimming now. When Greg gets off work, we can go again.

**Sue:** Good idea!

**Greg:** *[Walking away]* Forget it! You go swimming now. Be selfish. I've got to get to work.

**Carlos:** Boy, was he mad!

**Sue:** I guess so! He was mad just because he was going to be left out.

**Amber:** Let's get going! I'll see you back here in an hour.

| Skill | **37** | Being Assertive |

**Definition of Skill:**  Making a comment in a confident and firm manner, without making threats

**Skill Activities/ Discussions:**

1. Make a list of comments that includes polite, assertive, and aggressive remarks. Have the students determine which of the three types of comments they are. For example: *Polite*—"It's your bedtime. Would you please get into bed?" *Assertive*—"It is your bedtime. You need to get into bed now." *Aggressive*—"If you don't get into bed, you've had it!"

2. Prepare a list of situations that includes times when a polite comment would be appropriate and others when an assertive comment would be necessary. For example: *Polite*—Your teacher passed out scissors for a craft project and he accidentally gave you a pair for a left-handed person. You are not left-handed. *Assertive*—You bought a cassette player that came with a full one-year guarantee. One month later, it did not work. You asked the salesperson to replace it or fix it. The salesperson ignored the warranty and refused.

3. Have students compare the difference between being assertive and being aggressive.

**Situations:**  **Home**

You politely asked your younger sister to return your clothes clean and pressed after she borrows them, but she ignored you. Demonstrate how you would tell her again, in an assertive way.

**School**

A classmate continues to whisper to you during class and gets you in trouble. Demonstrate how you would ask him to stop. Use an assertive manner.

**Community**

You have asked your waitress for your bill three times, and she still hasn't brought it. Be assertive when you ask again.

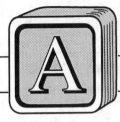

## Script A — Being Assertive

| | |
|---|---|
| **Number of Characters:** | 3 |
| **Character Description:** | Calley—A teenager |
| | Pat—Calley's older brother |
| | Mrs. Finley—Calley and Pat's mother |
| **Scene Description:** | Calley comes home from school and looks upset about something. Mrs. Finley and Pat decide to ask her what's wrong. |

**Pat:** Calley, what's your problem?

**Calley:** I don't know.

**Mrs. Finley:** You look upset about something. Do you feel like talking about it?

**Calley:** Oh, it's Becky. She makes me so mad!

**Mrs. Finley:** She's spreading more rumors, huh? Who is she picking on this time?

**Calley:** Me! She's telling stories about me that aren't true.

**Pat:** Rumors are kind of tough to deal with. How do you know she's doing it? Do you have proof?

**Calley:** You bet I do! I heard her myself. She didn't know I was in the locker room when she was talking about me to Jane and Kate.

**Pat:** What did she say?

**Calley:** She said that I cheat on tests and steal things.

**Pat:** Tell her if she doesn't stop lying, you'll mess up her face! Or better yet, tell her I will!

**Mrs. Finley:** Wait a minute. Why should Calley be aggressive? Then she'll be as bad as Becky! She shouldn't stoop to her level.

**Pat:** I guess not.

**Calley:** So what am I supposed to do?

**Mrs. Finley:** Have you talked to her about it yet?

**Calley:** No, I was too angry to talk.

**Mrs. Finley:** I'm glad you decided to cool down first. But I do think you ought to speak to her.

**Pat:** Calley can't exactly walk up to Becky and say, "Excuse me, Becky, but please stop spreading rumors about me, OK?"

**Calley:** Are you kidding? She'd laugh in my face and think I was weird.

**Mrs. Finley:** I think you should be assertive when you talk to her.

**Calley:** Say what?

**Mrs. Finley:** That means making a firm statement, without getting aggressive.

**Pat:** Yeah! Calley could say something like: "Becky, I heard you were spreading rumors about me yesterday. I don't appreciate it. I considered going to the principal, but I thought I should talk to you first."

**Calley:** That will really put her in her place, won't it?

**Mrs. Finley:** Hopefully, but if not, you may need to talk to one of your teachers or one of the counselors about it.

**Calley:** I'll talk to her tomorrow and see if it works. I don't know why she's always spreading rumors anyway.

*[They continue talking.]*

| **Number of Characters:** | 4 |
|---|---|
| **Character Description:** | Shannon—Decoration Committee chairperson |
| | Toni—Shannon's friend |
| | Steve—Committee member |
| | Renette—Committee member |
| **Scene Description:** | Shannon is the chairperson of the Decoration Committee for the school dance. The scene begins when her friend, Toni, asks her how the decorations are progressing. |

**Toni:** I can't wait to see you all dressed up at the dance this Friday. I'm really looking forward to it. How are the decorations coming?

**Shannon:** There are only three days left, and we aren't anywhere near finished yet.

**Toni:** I thought you split everything up between the people on your committee.

**Shannon:** I did. Everyone signed up for one job. That way I thought no one would end up doing too much.

**Toni:** So what's the problem?

**Shannon:** Well, a few of us have gotten our jobs finished, but most people on the committee haven't even started yet.

**Toni:** Like who?

**Shannon:** Look over there. Steve's just sitting around talking to his friends. He is supposed to make the swing for us.

*[Steve sees Shannon and walks up to her.]*

**Steve:** Hi, Toni! Hi, Shannon! Hey, Shannon, I wanted to tell you that I changed my mind about doing the swing. I won't be able to make it. Sorry.

**Shannon:** Oh, that's OK. Don't worry about it.

*[Steve walks away.]*

**Toni:** Shannon, you're such a pushover. Why didn't you let him know that it isn't OK for him to tell you three days before the dance?

**Shannon:** Well, I don't want to get bossy. Then people will get mad at me.

**Toni:** You need to be more assertive, Shannon, or I'm afraid you'll end up doing everything yourself.

**Shannon:** There's Renette. Let's go see if she has the table decorations done yet.

*[Toni and Shannon walk up to Renette.]*

**Shannon:** Hi, Renette. How are the centerpieces for the tables coming?

**Renette:** Not very well. I kept putting it off. Now I don't think I'm going to have any time to do it. Can you find someone else?

**Shannon:** Well, I was hoping I could count on you. It's sort of late to find some-body.

**Renette:** Oh, I'm sure you won't have any trouble. You're good at that sort of thing! See ya!

*[Renette walks away. Toni just shakes his head.]*

**Toni:** Shannon, you're just too nice. Being assertive doesn't mean being bossy.

**Shannon:** I wasn't any better that time, huh?

**Toni:** Well, put it this way. Who's going to end up doing the centerpieces?

**Shannon:** Me.

**Toni:** That's right, you!

## Skill 38     Making a Complaint

**Definition of Skill:**    Expressing dissatisfaction to whoever is responsible after not being satisfied with something

**Skill Activities/ Discussions:**

1. Have the students list situations when they would need to make complaints to parents, teachers, friends, store managers, etc.

2. Discuss the reasons why a person should not begin making a complaint in an aggressive manner. (See Skill #37.)

3. Discuss situations where a person may need to go from being polite to assertive when making a complaint. For example, a store clerk refuses to honor a warranty.

**Situations:**

**Home**

You share a bedroom with your brother or sister who has not been doing any of the cleaning. Demonstrate how you would make a complaint.

**School**

Your history teacher has been talking about the same Civil War battle for a week. Demonstrate how you could make a complaint to your teacher that class is boring.

**Community**

The local bowling alley does not have many light bowling balls for young people. As a result, your younger sister can never find a ball to use. Demonstrate how you could make a complaint to the manager.

| Number of Characters: | 4 |
|---|---|
| Character Description: | Martin—A teenage son |
| | Lena—Martin's younger sister |
| | Mr. Walker—Martin and Lena's father |
| | Mrs. Walker—Martin and Lena's mother |
| Scene Description: | The Walker family is having lunch. Martin has a complaint and decides this would be a good time to make it. |

**Martin:** Good lunch, Mom!

**Mrs. Walker:** Your father deserves all the credit. He made lunch while we were out shopping.

**Martin:** This was really good, Dad! Thanks. I love tacos!

**Mr. Walker:** I guess we better leave the meat warm on the stove. Ken will probably be starving when he gets home from the swim meet.

**Lena:** When is Ken going to come home?

*[Mrs. Walker stands up and starts picking up some of the plates.]*

**Mrs. Walker:** I'd say in about a half-hour. Well, Martin, this is your day to do the dishes. How about if I help you clear the table?

**Martin:** Thanks, Mom. Could you wait a minute though? I have something I want to talk about.

**Mr. Walker:** What's on your mind, Son?

*[Mrs. Walker puts the plates down and takes a seat at the table again.]*

**Martin:** Well, I guess I sort of have a complaint to make.

---

| | |
|---|---|
| **Lena:** | What's a complaint? |
| **Mr. Walker:** | It means that Martin is unhappy about something and he wants to tell us what he is dissatisfied with. |
| **Lena:** | I don't get it. |
| **Mrs. Walker:** | Lena, why don't we listen to Martin's complaint? Maybe that will help you understand it better. |
| **Martin:** | I could be wrong, but to me, it seems like the house chores are not split up very fairly among us. Don't get me wrong, I don't mind doing my part. But lately, it seems I'm the one doing the most. |
| **Mr. Walker:** | How do you think it's unfair? |
| **Martin:** | Well, I realize that Lena is still pretty young, but when I was her age, I had to do a few things! She still doesn't have any responsibilities around here! |
| **Lena:** | What's responsibility? |
| **Mrs. Walker:** | That's when you are in charge of doing something. Like today, it's Martin's responsibility to do the dishes. Is there anything else that makes it unfair, Martin? |
| **Martin:** | Yes, there is. Ken is so busy with sports, schoolwork, and clubs and stuff, that I can't remember the last time he's done anything around here. |
| **Mrs. Walker:** | Come to think of it, you're right, Martin. |
| **Martin:** | I'm getting pretty busy myself, but I still do my chores. I just don't think it's fair! |
| **Mrs. Walker:** | It really hasn't been fair, has it? Why don't we wait until Ken gets home, so we can talk about the problem together? |
| **Martin:** | OK. |

| Number of Characters: | 3 |
|---|---|
| Character Description: | Clay—A teenager |
| | Mrs. Brigham—Clay's mother |
| | Mr. Dobbs—Store clerk |
| Scene Description: | Clay and his mother are at the mall together, looking for a few things. |

**Mrs. Brigham:** Clay, I know you want to go into the electronics store to see if your order is in yet. Why don't you go ahead and I'll meet you there? I want to pick up a few cards.

**Clay:** That part for my stereo was supposed to be in three weeks ago. I'm getting tired of waiting.

**Mrs. Brigham:** I don't blame you. You've been waiting a long time for that part.

**Clay:** All together, it's been seven weeks since I first ordered it.

**Mrs. Brigham:** Well, you may need to make a complaint if it's not in yet. Do you know what I mean by *make a complaint?*

**Clay:** Oh, Mom! Of course, I do!

*[Clay leaves and goes to the electronics store. The store clerk reports that the part is still back-ordered.]*

**Clay:** I can't believe this! What kind of rinky-dink store is this anyway?

**Mr. Dobbs:** I apologize, sir. The company who makes that part has it on back-order. I called again, just last week, and they said it would be at least three more weeks. I'm sorry for the inconvenience.

**Clay:** You haven't called since last week? Why haven't you called this week? Or is that more than you can handle?

*[Mr. Dobbs looks annoyed and embarrassed
because Clay is talking so loudly.]*

**Mr. Dobbs:** The reason I didn't call again was because they told me that it would be at least three weeks more. I could call again now, if you'd like.

**Clay:** I don't want you to call. I just want the part. I'm sick of waiting.

*[Other customers in the store start looking
at Clay to see what he is yelling about.]*

**Clay:** I demand that you let me talk to your manager! Maybe he can give me some answers.

*[Clay's mother walks into the store and
overhears Clay's last few statements.]*

**Mr. Dobbs:** "He" is a "she." The store manager is Ms. Cleaver. But she is on her lunch break and won't be back for about 15 minutes.

**Mrs. Brigham:** Please excuse my son's rude behavior. We'll come back when the manager is in.

*[Mrs. Brigham and Clay leave the store.]*

**Clay:** But, Mom, I was just making a complaint like you told me to.

**Mrs. Brigham:** Clay, you're not being assertive. You're being rude. There's a big difference.

*[Mrs. Brigham continues to talk to
Clay about how to be assertive.]*

**Definition of Skill:** Listening to someone express dissatisfaction about something you are responsible for accomplishing

**Skill Activities/ Discussions:**

1. List things that teenagers may do that would cause people to complain to them (e.g., chewing gum too loudly).

2. Talk about why stores have customer service desks to handle complaints.

3. Discuss why people sometimes get defensive when they receive a complaint.

**Situations:**

**Home**

You are having a party. Your neighbors tell you that the music is too loud and they can't get to sleep. Demonstrate how you should respond to their complaint.

**School**

You are taking a test and don't realize that you are tapping your pencil until the person next to you makes a complaint. Demonstrate how you would respond.

**Community**

You and your friends ride your bikes to the swimming pool and leave them in the entrance. You receive a complaint from the lifeguard that your bikes are in the way. Show how you should respond.

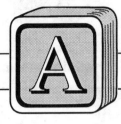
| Number of Characters: | 2 |
| --- | --- |
| Character Description: | Ben—A teenager |
| | Ruth—Ben's younger sister |
| Scene Description: | It is Saturday afternoon. Ben and Ruth are home alone. |

**Ruth:** Ben, I'm bored! Will you do something with me?

**Ben:** I guess so. What do you want to do?

**Ruth:** How about watch TV?

**Ben:** Nah. There's nothing good on Saturday afternoon.

**Ruth:** Let's play video games.

**Ben:** OK. That sounds great!

> *[They go into the family room to set up the video player.]*

**Ben:** Can I go first?

**Ruth:** Yeah. I don't know how to play this one anyway. If you go first, then I can watch.

**Ben:** Levels one and two are pretty easy. But wait till you see level three! It's wild! You have to wait until I get through level three before you can try, OK?

**Ruth:** How long is it going to take you?

**Ben:** Not long. I'm a whiz at this game!

> *[Ben gets through level one and two without losing a man. But he has problems with level three and the game is over.]*

**Ruth:** I think I got it. Let me try now.

**Ben:** No way! You said I could play till I got through level three.

**Ruth:** Oh, yeah. I guess I did.

> *[Ben really gets into the game, but has a hard time getting through level three. Ruth tries to be as patient as she can, but finally decides to complain to Ben.]*

**Ruth:** Ben, I've been waiting about 20 minutes. I'd really like to have a turn.

**Ben:** Let me have one more try. I think I can make it this time.

**Ruth:** Ben, you've been saying that for the last five minutes. When I agreed to let you play through level three, you said it wouldn't take you long. I think I've waited long enough. I'd like to have a turn now.

> *[Ben can tell that he is receiving a sincere complaint from his sister, by the look on her face.]*

**Ben:** OK, I guess you have been waiting long enough.

**Ruth:** Finally! Now, I'll show you how to get through level three.

**Ben:** No way! Not on your first try.

**Ruth:** Just watch and see.

> *[Ben and Ruth continue playing the video game.]*

| | |
|---|---|
| **Number of Characters:** | 3 |
| **Character Description:** | Kari—A student |
| | Mr. Olski—Kari's math teacher |
| | Bart—A student |
| **Scene Description:** | Kari is in math class. She is having a difficult time concentrating because she is so thirsty. The class is almost over, but she decides that she can't wait. The scene begins when Kari raises her hand. |

**Mr. Olski:** Yes, Kari?

**Kari:** I'm really thirsty. May I get a drink?

**Mr. Olski:** Yes, but do it quietly, please.

*[Kari leaves the classroom.]*

**Mr. Olski:** I like how you're all using this class time to get started on your homework assignment.

*[Kari comes back into the room. On her way back to her seat, she disrupts the class by cracking a joke and punching another student in the arm.]*

**Mr. Olski:** Kari, please sit down quietly. I'd like everyone to keep working until the bell rings.

**Kari:** *[Whispering]* What's his problem? All he does is yell!

**Bart:** *[Whispering]* He wasn't yelling. He was making a complaint. You know, he could have told you to wait until the bell rang to get your drink of water. He did ask you to come back in quietly.

**Kari:** *[Whispering louder]* Come off it! He just likes to yell, especially at me!

**Mr. Olski:** I asked you to quiet down, Kari. Since you've wasted two minutes of our time, now you owe me two minutes after class.

> *[The bell rings and the kids get up to leave.*
> *Kari walks over to Mr. Olski's desk.]*

**Kari:** How come you only yell at the things I do, and you never yell at anyone else?

**Mr. Olski:** Kari, I wasn't yelling. I asked you to get a drink quietly and you didn't. I was making a complaint.

> *[Kari waits her two minutes and then leaves the room.]*

**Skill** **40** **Giving Negative Feedback**

**Definition of Skill:** Letting a person know in a constructive way what was done wrong

**Skill Activities/ Discussions:**

1. Give students a list of "put-downs" and have them change them into constructive comments. For example, "Your eye contact is lousy" could be changed to "I feel that your eye contact could be improved."

2. Have students list situations when they may need to give a critique of another person. Define *critique* for students if necessary.

3. Discuss reasons why it is important to be understanding and concerned when giving negative feedback rather than being "bossy."

**Situations:**

**Home**

Sometimes your younger brother dresses funny because he has trouble matching clothes. Demonstrate how you could give him negative feedback about the way he dresses.

**School**

Your teacher asks you to evaluate her teaching at the end of the school year. You think that she talks too much. Demonstrate how you would tell her, in a constructive way.

**Community**

Your scout leader asks how you feel about the way he is running things. You think he doesn't plan enough fun activities. Show how you would give negative feedback.

| | |
|---|---|
| **Number of Characters:** | 3 |
| **Character Description:** | Paul—A friend |
| | Kimberly—A friend |
| | Frank—A friend |
| **Scene Description:** | Kimberly and Frank are in English class together. They have an assignment to put on a skit in front of their class. The scene begins when Kimberly and Frank are telling Paul about it. |

**Paul:** It seems like you two have been working a long time on the skit. I bet you'll get a good grade!

**Kimberly:** After all this, we better!

**Paul:** When do you present this masterpiece?

**Frank:** Day after tomorrow. We're even going to have props. I hope the rest of the class likes it.

**Kimberly:** The only thing that worries me is that we've spent all our time writing it. We haven't even acted it out yet.

**Paul:** Why don't you act it out now?

**Frank:** Would you give us a critique, Paul, and tell us what you think?

**Paul:** Sure! I'd like to see it!

*[As Paul watches, he notices that Kimberly is talking too fast and feels he should say something. He waits until they are finished.]*

**Kimberly:** Well, Paul, how did you like it?

**Paul:** I thought it was great! It was funny and really kept my attention.

**Frank:** I'm glad you liked it.

**Paul:** Kimberly, I like your eye contact and your volume was very good. I think that you need to slow down. If you talk too fast, the kids might miss some of the jokes. Do you know what I mean?

**Kimberly:** I sure do. I didn't realize I was talking that fast.

**Frank:** Right before we go up in front of the class, let's remind each other not to talk too fast. I tend to do that too, especially if I get nervous. What do you think?

**Kimberly:** I think that's a good idea.

**Paul:** Thanks for letting me watch your skit. I really enjoyed it. What props are you going to use?

**Frank:** We haven't actually decided yet.

**Kimberly:** Let's go over to my house. We have lots of stuff in our basement.

*[The three of them leave and go to Kimberly's house.]*

| | |
|---|---|
| **Number of Characters:** | 3 |
| **Character Description:** | Aldo—A teenager |
| | Mr. Busot—Aldo's father |
| | Ms. Spring—Aldo's student teacher |
| **Scene Description:** | Aldo and his father are at a flea market and Aldo's student teacher is there also. |

**Aldo:** Hey, Dad, there's Ms. Spring. She's the new student teacher I was telling you about.

**Mr. Busot:** Oh, yeah? Is she a good teacher?

**Aldo:** Pretty good. The kids really like her.

**Mr. Busot:** Will she be at your school all semester?

**Aldo:** I'm not sure how long she'll be there.

*[Ms. Spring recognizes Aldo and walks over to say hi.]*

**Ms. Spring:** Hello, Aldo! I'm so new in this city, it's nice to see a familiar face.

**Aldo:** Hello, Ms. Spring! This is my dad, Mr. Busot. Dad, this is Ms. Spring, our student teacher in math class.

**Mr. Busot:** It's a pleasure to meet you! How do you like the school?

**Ms. Spring:** The teachers are very friendly. The kids are pretty well-behaved. Since this is my first time, I wasn't sure if the students would be able to understand my teaching.

**Mr. Busot:** I'll bet it was difficult getting up in front of the class for the first time!

**Ms. Spring:** It really was. I don't know, how do you think I'm doing, Aldo?

**Aldo:** You've got to be more strict. Some of the kids are getting away with a lot.

| | |
|---|---|
| **Ms. Spring:** | That's a good suggestion, Aldo! I'll see if I can work on that. |
| **Aldo:** | I'd slow down if I were you. Sometimes you talk too fast. Oh, and another thing. We're not used to having so much homework. You should ease up a bit. |
| **Ms. Spring:** | *[Looking disappointed]* I guess I have a lot to work on, don't I? I'd better let you two get back to your shopping. It was nice to meet you, Mr. Busot. Aldo, I'll see you Monday. Bye. |
| **Aldo:** | Bye, Ms. Spring. |
| **Mr. Busot:** | Boy, Aldo, you really gave her a lot of negative comments. I thought you told me the kids really like her. |
| **Aldo:** | Well, they do! I just thought I should point a few things out. |
| **Mr. Busot:** | I think that's good, except you didn't tell her anything positive. I think she left feeling like her teaching methods are all wrong. |
| **Aldo:** | I see what you mean. I'll meet you here in a few minutes. I'm going to see if I can find her and apologize. |

# Skill 41     Accepting Negative Feedback

**Definition of Skill:**    Accepting constructive criticism and responding appropriately

**Skill Activities/ Discussions:**

1. Discuss the reasons why it is sometimes difficult to accept negative feedback.

2. Present situations where negative feedback is given and ask the students how they feel.

3. Have students compare how *receiving a complaint* is different from *accepting negative feedback.*

**Situations:**

**Home**

Your parents are happy that you did all your chores on Saturday, but they are concerned about the way you cleaned the bathroom. Show how you would respond to their negative feedback.

**School**

Your teacher points out a weakness in the character description in your story. Demonstrate how you should accept this negative feedback.

**Community**

The Schaeffers really like you as a babysitter. However, they tell you that you shouldn't feed the kids so much "junk food." Demonstrate how you would respond.

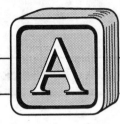

| | |
|---|---|
| **Number of Characters:** | 3 |
| **Character Description:** | April—A teenager |
| | Mr. Detert—April's father |
| | Mrs. Detert—April's mother |
| **Scene Description:** | The scene begins when April and her parents are discussing her report card. |

| | |
|---|---|
| **April:** | We got our report cards in school today. |
| **Mrs. Detert:** | You've been spending a lot of time doing your schoolwork the last couple of months. I'll bet your grades are pretty good. |
| | *[April smiles and hands her grades to her parents.]* |
| **Mr. Detert:** | Wow! They really are good, April! I see you've improved in a couple of classes. |
| **April:** | Well, I wasn't too happy with my grades in science and history last time, so I really concentrated on those two classes. |
| **Mrs. Detert:** | I see that. You got a "B+" in science and a "B-" in history. What did you have last time? |
| **April:** | *[Feeling proud]* A "C-" in science and a "D+" in history. |
| **Mr. Detert:** | You brought up both grades quite a bit, April. That shows a lot of hard work on your part. You must feel pretty good about your accomplishments! |
| **April:** | Yeah. I guess I do. |
| **Mrs. Detert:** | I am concerned about your math grade, though. I think it went down, didn't it? |

**April:** You're right. Last time I had an "A" and now it's a "C+." I'm not really sure why it dropped so much.

**Mrs. Detert:** Maybe you were working so hard at science and history that your math didn't always get finished.

**April:** You're right. I'll see if I can divide my time a little more equally this quarter.

**Mrs. Detert:** We're really proud of the way you improved in science and history. I think this report card deserves a little celebration. Let's go out for some ice cream.

**April:** Great! Where should we go?

*[The Deterts leave for the ice cream parlor.]*

| | |
|---|---|
| **Number of Characters:** | 2 |
| **Character Description:** | Wess—A teenager |
| | Mr. Dunkin—Wess's manager |
| **Scene Description:** | Wess works at a fast-food restaurant. The scene begins when Mr. Dunkin, the manager, calls Wess into his office. |

**Mr. Dunkin:** Wess, do you remember when I hired you? I told you that I would be evaluating you after you'd been working three months.

**Wess:** Yes, sir, I do.

**Mr. Dunkin:** That's why I asked you to come in. I'd like to do that now. Can you believe it's been three months already?

**Wess:** No, I can't! Time sure flies. It seems like I just started a week ago.

**Mr. Dunkin:** Wess, I must say that I'm very glad to have you working for us. You're doing a find job!

**Wess:** Thank you, sir. I really like this job.

*[Wess smiles and is glad to be hearing good things.]*

**Mr. Dunkin:** I like the way you are always on time and how polite you are to the customers. These are good qualities.

**Wess:** Well, I try to do my best.

**Mr. Dunkin:** However, I would like to work on improving your appearance. I think . . .

**Wess:** *[Interrupting]* What do you mean, improve my appearance? What's wrong with my appearance?

**Mr. Dunkin:** I was trying to tell you, before you interrupted. Oftentimes, you come to work in a dirty uniform, and your hair is uncombed and sometimes dirty. Do you understand what I'm getting at?

**Wess:** Are you trying to tell me that my job performance doesn't mean anything? The only thing that counts around here is that I look good?

**Mr. Dunkin:** No, that's not what I'm saying. Your job performance is very important and I've told you that you're doing very well. But, appearance is also important, especially when you are serving food to people.

**Wess:** You have me working so many hours, I don't have time to wash my clothes.

*[Mr. Dunkin is surprised and disappointed in the way Wess is reacting to the negative feedback.]*

**Mr. Dunkin:** I can understand you must be busy going to school and working too. Perhaps ordering a few more uniforms would help.

**Wess:** Yeah, right! On the money I make at this place, I don't think I can afford it.

**Mr. Dunkin:** I want you to evaluate whether you really want to work here or not. If you do, then I expect you to work on improving your appearance.

*[Wess leaves Mr. Dunkin's office, not realizing how inappropriate his behavior was.]*

## Skill 42 — Dealing with a False Accusation

**Definition of Skill:** Dealing with being blamed for doing something you have not done

**Skill Activities/ Discussions:**

1. Discuss possible reasons why one person may falsely accuse another person (e.g., not having all the facts, jumping to conclusions).

2. Have the students discuss if and when they have been falsely accused. When they have been falsely accused, how have they offered proof that they didn't do it? Is different proof needed in different situations?

3. Discuss our judicial system and the concept of being innocent until proven guilty. How does that relate to being falsely accused?

**Situations:**

**Home**
Your brother has accused you of taking money from his wallet, but you didn't do it. Demonstrate how you would deal with this situation.

**School**
You were seen in the hall shortly before the trophy case was broken. You are being blamed for the incident, but you are really innocent. Demonstrate what you should say or do in this situation.

**Community**
You are captain of a softball team. Your team is being falsely blamed for the disappearance of the plates from the infield. Demonstrate how you would deal with this situation.

# Script A — Dealing with a False Accusation

| | |
|---|---|
| **Number of Characters:** | 3 |
| **Character Description:** | Mrs. Chang—A librarian |
| | Marty—A teenager |
| | Whitney—Marty's friend |
| **Scene Description:** | Marty signs into the library during his study hall. He just sits down in the back of the library, when the librarian calls him up to the desk. |

**Marty:** Hello, Mrs. Chang.

**Mrs. Chang:** Hello, Marty. Do you by chance have the book *Treasure Island* here with you?

**Marty:** No, I don't.

**Mrs. Chang:** According to my records, you were the last person to check out the book and it's a month overdue. We've started a new policy that says any student with an overdue book isn't allowed to come in during a study hall. So, I'm afraid I have to ask you to sign out. See if you can bring the book back later today or tomorrow morning, so that you can use the library again during study halls.

**Marty:** I think there has been some mistake. The reason I don't have the book with me is because I finished it and turned it back in a couple weeks ago. Maybe it was put back on the shelf in the wrong place.

**Mrs. Chang:** Before we put a book back on the shelf, the card is put back inside the cover. You can see I have the card with your signature right here. That's why I believe that it never was brought back. Why don't you go look in your locker and see if it's in there?

**Marty:** I'm certain I returned it. In fact, I have proof. I put it in the book drop with my friend, Whitney. She returned a book the same time I did.

**Mrs. Chang:** Is her name Whitney Richards?

**Marty:** Yes, she is sitting right over there.

**Mrs. Chang:** Well, I was going to call her to my desk next, because she also has an overdue book.

**Marty:** I wonder if it's the book she returned along with mine that day?

**Mrs. Chang:** Good question. Why don't you go get her and we'll ask?

*[Marty goes to get Whitney and explains the situation. They both come up to Mrs. Chang's desk.]*

**Whitney:** I'll vouch for Marty. I saw him put the book in the book return slot, the same time I returned *The Secret Cabin*.

**Mrs. Chang:** Well, this is strange. I still have the card from that book too.

**Whitney:** You know, the library is usually locked up by 4:30, right?

**Mrs. Chang:** That's correct.

**Whitney:** Marty, do you remember if it was around 5:00 the day we returned the books?

**Marty:** That's right, I remember now. We expected the doors to be locked, but they weren't. They were still open.

**Whitney:** Yeah, only the lights were turned off. So we used the book drop anyway.

**Mrs. Chang:** I apologize for falsely accusing you two. I think you have given me ample proof to show that something else has happened to those books. Thank you for trying to help me solve this mystery. I'll look into it further and let you know what I find out. Thank you.

**Marty:** Bye, Mrs. Chang. I hope you find them.

| Number of Characters: | 3 |
|---|---|
| Character Description: | Vanna—A salesclerk |
| | Dick—A salesclerk |
| | Mr. Houston—The boss |
| Scene Description: | Vanna and Dick both work at a fast-food restaurant. Someone stole money from the office. Vanna and Dick are both innocent. The scene begins when Vanna is checking in to start work. |

**Vanna:** Hi, Dick! I didn't know we were scheduled to work together again today.

**Dick:** We sure are.

**Vanna:** I hope it's not busy today. I'm kind of tired.

**Dick:** I wouldn't count on it. Did you hear what happened last night while we were working?

**Vanna:** No, what?

**Dick:** Someone stole money out of the office.

**Vanna:** You've got to be kidding! Who would do a thing like that?

**Dick:** I don't know.

**Vanna:** You know, I had to go into the office last night to get some change. When I came out, Roger went in.

**Dick:** I wonder what he was doing in there?

*[Mr. Houston comes out of the office and walks over to Dick and Vanna.]*

**Mr. Houston:** Hello. Say, Vanna, before you begin work, I would like to talk to you in my office. When we're finished, you can take over Dick's station as I'd like to talk to him also.

*[Vanna glances at Dick with a worried look on her face and then follows Mr. Houston into his office.]*

**Mr. Houston:** I'd like you to tell me what station you worked last night, and if you were by any chance in this office at all.

**Vanna:** I heard about the money being stolen. You think I did it, don't you? I can't believe you think I took it!

**Mr. Houston:** Vanna, I have witnesses who said they saw you in the office last night.

**Vanna:** You must think I took the money. I can't believe this. After working here for over a year and never being late once, you think I did it?

**Mr. Houston:** Vanna, could you tell me why you were in the office last night?

**Vanna:** Why should I tell you anything? It won't do any good anyway. You already think I did it. Maybe I should just quit, if I can't be trusted.

*[Mr. Houston finds Vanna's behavior to be very suspicious. He decides to question her again later, after she cools down.]*

**Mr. Houston:** Vanna, why don't we continue this conversation later? Please ask Dick to come in next.

*[Vanna is outraged because she thinks she is being falsely accused and storms out of Mr. Houston's office.]*

# Skill 43 — Making an Accusation

**Definition of Skill:** Blaming someone for doing something wrong

**Skill Activities/ Discussions:**

1. Prepare and read to the students a story that sounds as if one person did something wrong. Ask the students to make an accusation based on the information given to them. Next, give additional information about the situation which shows that someone else did it. Discuss the idea that things are not always what they seem.

2. Discuss why it is important to gather all the facts before making an accusation.

3. Discuss what can be considered proof in different situations.

**Situations:**

**Home**
One of your friends saw your younger brother (sister) wearing your favorite shirt downtown. You go to your closet and it is gone. Demonstrate how you would make an accusation to your brother (sister).

**School**
Your best friend hears another person spreading an untrue rumor about you. Show how you would accuse the person of spreading rumors.

**Community**
You see two kids shoplifting at a local store. Demonstrate how you could make an accusation to the store manager.

| | |
|---|---|
| **Number of Characters:** | 3 |
| **Character Description:** | Paula—A teenager |
| | Tom—A teenager |
| | Ryan—The class bully |
| **Scene Description:** | Paula and Tom are riding their bikes to the roller-skating rink. The scene begins as they are arriving and find Ryan waiting in the parking lot. |

**Paula:** Oh, great! Look who's over by the door. It drives me crazy how Ryan is always trying to push people around.

**Tom:** I really don't trust that guy. Let's just try to get past him quickly.

*[As Paula and Tom are putting their bikes in the rack, Ryan walks over.]*

**Ryan:** Hey, Tom! I see you have a new bike. Let me take it for a spin.

**Tom:** I don't think so, Ryan. Since it's new, I'm not letting anyone use it.

**Ryan:** You don't think so, do you? You know if I want to ride your bike, I don't think you can stop me.

**Paula:** Knock it off, Ryan. Go bug someone else. We're really not interested.

*[Paula and Tom go inside to skate. When they come out, Tom's bike is not in the rack.]*

**Tom:** I can't believe this! A brand new bike, and it's stolen. Why didn't I lock it up?

**Paula:** I guess Ryan had us so upset that we forgot. I wonder why my bike wasn't taken too?

**Tom:** I better call the police right away. Are you thinking what I'm thinking about Ryan?

---

**Paula:** I sure am. I think he took it. All the evidence points to him.

**Tom:** Yeah, but we really don't have any proof yet that he actually did take it. When I call the police, I don't think I know enough to actually accuse him, do you?

**Paula:** No, I suppose not. But that can't stop us from checking around to look for proof.

**Tom:** While I call the police, would you mind going back in and asking around?

**Paula:** Not at all. Maybe we can even go by Ryan's house to see if the bike is over there.

| | |
|---|---|
| **Number of Characters:** | 3 |
| **Character Description:** | Jacob—A teenager |
| | Mr. Simon—Jacob's father |
| | Mrs. Simon—Jacob's mother |
| **Scene Description:** | The Simon's teenage son, Jacob, has been hinting to his parents that he really wants a CD player for his birthday. He knows that it is expensive, and is willing to help pay for part of it. Mr. and Mrs. Simon are in their bedroom, talking about whether or not they can afford the CD player for Jacob. Jacob knows what they are talking about. He attempts to block out their talking by playing with the family's new seven-week-old puppy, Pepsi. |

| | |
|---|---|
| **Mrs. Simon:** | Well, what do you think about getting a CD player for Jacob's birthday? |
| **Mr. Simon:** | I think that if we got him anything else, he would be pretty disappointed. |
| **Mrs. Simon:** | He has been talking about it for months now. |
| **Mr. Simon:** | It will be more expensive than we usually pay for birthdays, but I think he deserves it! |
| **Mrs. Simon:** | I agree. He's really been working hard at school all year. |
| **Mr. Simon:** | If we get it before his birthday, he'll find it, you know. |
| **Mrs. Simon:** | Why don't you pick it up at the mall after work, the day of his birthday? We'll surprise him at dinner! |
| **Mr. Simon:** | I'll pick up one of the wicker dog beds for Pepsi at the same time. I've been meaning to get one for him. |

*[Jacob happens to walk by his parents' bedroom and can't help but overhear their conversation.]*

| | |
|---|---|
| **Mrs. Simon:** | I don't think I would spend that kind of money on him yet. He'll probably just wreck it. |

**Mr. Simon:** I guess he is a bit young. Maybe we should wait a couple of years to get one for him. We'll be able to trust him more not to be so reckless when he's older.

*[Jacob can't believe what he is hearing! He thinks his parents are saying those things about him. He can't stand to listen to any more comments and leaves to go to his room.]*

**Mrs. Simon:** In the meantime, Pepsi can just sleep on some old towels. I can't wait to see Jacob's face when he opens his gift!

**Mr. Simon:** Me, neither.

*[The next day at breakfast, Jacob is very quiet. His parents can tell his is upset about something.]*

**Mr. Simon:** Jacob, you look upset this morning. Is something bothering you?

**Jacob:** I guess not.

*[Mrs. Simon tries to talk about something positive.]*

**Mrs. Simon:** Jacob, would you mind waiting to celebrate at dinner time on your birthday?

**Jacob:** I guess it doesn't really matter. Since you both think I'm so reckless and hate to spend money on me! I guess I won't have much to look forward to.

**Mr. Simon:** Wait a minute! Just what are you accusing us of?

**Jacob:** I heard what you were saying about me in your room last night, and how I'm not going to get the CD player.

*[Mr. and Mrs. Simon look puzzled.]*

**Mrs. Simon:** You don't suppose he heard us talking about Pepsi and not getting him a dog bed, do you?

*[The three of them realize what happened and start laughing.]*

| Skill | **44** | Compromising/Negotiating |

**Definition of Skill:** Reaching acceptable agreements through talking, with each person giving in a little

**Skill Activities/ Discussions:**

1. Ask students to describe situations when they have disagreed with their parents and how they came to an agreement.

2. Ask students how they feel about a person who always has to have his way and is unwilling to "bend" a little.

3. Prepare and read situations where there is a disagreement between two people. Tell them what ended up happening. Have the students determine if any compromising occurred.

**Situations:**

**Home**

Your parents want you home by 9:00. All your friends stay out until 10:00. Demonstrate how you and your parents could negotiate.

**School**

The school has a policy that says students are only allowed at their lockers before and after school. The student council believes that students should be allowed to go to their lockers in between their classes. Propose a reasonable compromise.

**Community**

Your friend wants to spend the day fishing and you want to go shopping. Show how you could compromise.

| | |
|---|---|
| **Number of Characters:** | 3 |
| **Character Description:** | Shelly—A teenager |
| | Mike—Shelly's younger brother |
| | Mr. Zigler—Shelly and Mike's father |
| **Scene Description:** | Shelly's parents are going out of town for the weekend. The scene begins when Shelly hangs up the phone after talking to her best friend, McKinzey. |

**Shelly:** I don't think they'll mind. They trust me. I better check with my parents, just to make sure it's OK. I'll call you back, McKinzey. Bye.

**Mike:** I didn't mean to listen in on your conversation, Shelly, but I couldn't help it. There's no way Mom and Dad are going to let you have a party this weekend when they're not around.

**Shelly:** Why won't they? I'm a responsible person. They trust me.

**Mike:** I'm telling you, there's no way.

**Shelly:** Well, I guess I'll just have to go find out, won't I?

*[Shelly goes downstairs and finds her dad reading a magazine.]*

**Shelly:** Dad, do you have a minute? I'd like to ask you something.

**Mr. Zigler:** Sure! What's on your mind?

**Shelly:** Well, I was just talking to McKinzey on the phone. Since you and Mom are going away this weekend, we thought it would be fun to have a party here Saturday night. We'd have maybe 20 kids over, make some pizzas, and rent some movies.

**Mr. Zigler:** I don't know about that, Shelly. I'm afraid I can't let you do it when we're not here.

**Shelly:** *[Looking very disappointed]* I thought you trusted me, Dad. I can handle it!

**Mr. Zigler:** I know you could handle it. I do trust you! Just the fact that you're asking permission shows a lot of responsibility. The problem is, you can't be responsible for the other 20 kids' actions. There really has to be adult supervision.

**Shelly:** I can't believe this! Could I at least have McKinzey over? We could still have pizza and a movie.

**Mr. Zigler:** That sounds like a fair compromise! McKinzey's parents need to know that we won't be here, though.

**Shelly:** OK, I'll go call McKinzey.

> *[Shelly goes back upstairs to call. She hopes that she doesn't run into Mike. She doesn't feel like hearing, "I told you so."]*

| | |
|---|---|
| **Number of Characters:** | 4 |
| **Character Description:** | Victor—The class president |
| | Ann—The class vice-president |
| | Jake—A student |
| | Courtney—A student |
| **Scene Description:** | The class is meeting to plan their hall decorations during School Spirit Week. |

**Victor:** Does anyone have any good ideas for decorating our hall?

**Jake:** I think we should set up strobe lights. I know a couple of kids who have them. We could paint our signs with "glow in the dark" paint and turn the lights off before school, when the teachers are judging.

**Ann:** I like that idea! I can't remember anyone ever doing that before. I think we could win first place for originality.

**Victor:** I agree. Any other ideas?

**Courtney:** I was thinking we could have an old-fashioned theme. We can do all the posters in old-fashioned lettering. You know, the girls could wear long skirts and things like that.

**Jake:** You've got to be kidding!

**Victor:** Now, wait a minute, Jake. Her ideas have originality, too. We need to hear everyone's ideas. Are there any others?

*[No one offers more ideas, so Victor decides to have people vote between the two suggestions.]*

**Victor:** All those who would like to use Jake's idea, raise your hands.

**Ann:** Excuse me, Victor. I'm sorry to interrupt, but I just thought of an idea that would include both Courtney's and Jake's suggestions.

**Courtney:** Sounds interesting. What is it?

**Ann:** How about if we have the slogan "Past, Present, and Future—We'll Always Be the Best!" The hall could be divided into three sections. Jake's strobes could be used in the future section and Courtney's ideas for the past. The present section obviously wouldn't be any problem!

**Victor:** That sounds like a good compromise, so we can use both ideas. How do the rest of you feel about it?

**Courtney:** I like the idea!

*[The majority of the class agrees, but Jake hasn't said anything.]*

**Ann:** Jake, how do you feel about this?

**Jake:** I think you guys are going to compromise us all the way out of first place and right into last. I say we go with my original idea or I don't want anything to do with it.

**Victor:** We better vote. Majority rules.

*[The class begins to vote again. Jake can see the class is going to pick the "Past-Present-Future" theme. He leaves the meeting before anyone can ask him to get the strobe lights.]*

## Skill 45 — Accepting Consequences

**Definition of Skill:** Being able to face what happens as a result of an action

**Skill Activities/ Discussions:**

1. Have the students try to think of an action that does not have any consequences. (Conclusion: Every action has a consequence.)

2. Ask the students to make two lists. The first list should contain actions and their possible positive consequences (e.g., studying may result in good grades), and the second list should contain actions and their possible negative consequences.

3. Ask the students to list different negative and positive consequences they face at home, at school, and in the community.

**Situations:**

**Home**

You knew that if you stayed out past 10:00 you would be punished, but you did it anyway. Demonstrate how you would accept the consequences from your parents.

**School**

You knew that if you got excellent grades, you could be awarded a scholarship to go on to school. Your dream came true. Show how you would accept that consequence of your actions.

**Community**

You knew that reckless skating was not allowed at the skating rink. Sure enough, when you got wild, the manager asked you to leave. Accept the consequences of your actions.

| | |
|---|---|
| **Number of Characters:** | 3 |
| **Character Description:** | Jackie—A teenager |
| | Mr. Barent—Jackie's father |
| | Mrs. Barent—Jackie's mother |
| **Scene Description:** | Jackie wanted to drive her parents' car over to her boyfriend's house to say good-bye before he left on vacation. She knew that she had to ask permission to use the car, but her parents were gone. If she didn't leave right away, she would miss her boyfriend. Jackie decided to take the car and take her chances. The scene begins when Jackie comes back home and sees that her parents are there. |

**Jackie:** Hi, Mom! Hi, Dad!

**Mr. Barent:** You know how we feel about you taking the car without permission. I thought we made that quite clear to you.

*[Jackie knows that she has to accept the consequences of her actions.]*

**Jackie:** Yes, I do know. I took the car over to John's house to say good-bye to him before he left on vacation.

**Mr. Barent:** Why couldn't you just say good-bye over the phone? You saw him last night!

**Jackie:** That's not the same, Dad. I just had to say good-bye one more time. I was wrong to take the car without asking. I'm sorry.

**Mrs. Barent:** You know this means one month without the car. We discussed the consequences of taking the car without asking before this even happened.

**Jackie:** Yes, I know. I really do apologize. It won't happen again.

**Mr. Barent:** I hope not.

**Jackie:** I better go see what kind of shape my bike is in.

## Script B — Accepting Consequences

| Number of Characters: | 3 |
|---|---|
| **Character Description:** | Paul—A teenager |
| | Toby—Paul's friend |
| | Coach O'Brien—Paul's coach |
| **Scene Description:** | Paul meets Toby at his locker after school. |

**Paul:** Hey, Toby! Let's run down to the arcade and play a few games.

**Toby:** Sounds good! But you've got basketball practice, don't you?

**Paul:** Yeah, but if we get right down there, I'll only be about 15 minutes late.

**Toby:** I thought you said that if you were late again, Coach O'Brien was going to bench you.

**Paul:** That's what he said, but I don't think he meant it. Come on, let's go. I made a bet in science that I could break 4000 and I need you as my witness.

**Toby:** OK, if you say so.

*[It takes Paul longer than he thinks to break the score and he ends up a half-hour late for practice. When he shows up, Paul can tell Coach O'Brien is irritated.]*

**Coach O'Brien:** Paul, can I see you for a minute? Do you remember I told you that you'd be benched if you were late again?

**Paul:** You weren't serious, were you?

**Coach O'Brien:** Of course, I was serious!

**Paul:** Oh, come on. I wasn't that late!

**Coach O'Brien:** Practice started 35 minutes ago, Paul! We have to work together as a team to do well. It's not fair to the other people who get here on time every night.

**Paul:**    Give me a break, Coach! Please? I'll stay late and practice today.

**Coach O'Brien:**    I'm sorry, Paul, but you are benched for one week. And you won't be able to play in Friday night's game.

**Paul:**    I won't? That's not fair!

**Coach O'Brien:**    Fair? You had fair warning and took your chances. What's *not* fair is that you let your teammates down. Now they can't count on you in the game on Friday. I want you to think about the consequences of your actions.

**Paul:**    I don't believe this is happening. I just don't believe it.

*[Paul heads for the locker room to get dressed again.]*

| Skill | **46** | Expressing Feelings |

**Definition of Skill:** Telling about different emotions to another person

**Skill Activities/ Discussions:**

1. Have the students brainstorm a list of as many different emotion words they can think of. Compare the body language and facial expressions that are related to each feeling.

2. Discuss what happens when feelings are held inside. For example, someone may end up exploding, sometimes at a person who should not be involved.

3. Compare positive and negative ways of expressing feelings.

4. Discuss why feelings are sometimes difficult to identify. Discuss what the phrase *mixed emotions* means.

**Situations:**

**Home**

Your mom decides to get a job at night after being home full-time for five years. You're having mixed feelings about it. Demonstrate how you could express those feelings.

**School**

You have a lot of strong feelings when you think about graduating from school. Show how you would talk about those feelings.

**Community**

You have negative feelings about the city's tearing up one of the park's ball fields for an office building. Express those feelings.

| **Number of Characters:** | 2 |
|---|---|
| **Character Description:** | Carl—A teenager |
| | Adam—Carl's friend |
| **Scene Description:** | Adam notices that Carl has not been himself for awhile. The scene begins when Adam decides to talk to Carl about it. |

**Adam:** Hey, buddy! What's happening?

**Carl:** Not much, I guess.

**Adam:** What do you have planned this weekend? How would you like to go see that movie that's supposed to be so good? You know the one I'm talking about? I can't think of the name.

**Carl:** No, thanks. I think I'm just going to stay around home this weekend.

**Adam:** You know, Carl, we've been friends for a long time. I can tell something is wrong. What's up?

**Carl:** I guess I'm not exactly sure.

**Adam:** Well, if you need someone to talk to, let me know.

**Carl:** I guess it's just hard to know where to start.

**Adam:** Start with what's bugging you.

**Carl:** I don't think it's any one thing, Adam, or I could figure out what's bugging me. I think it's everything in general . . . school, my dad losing his job. You know.

**Adam:** Sometimes I get that way, too. It's like I can't understand how I'm feeling about anything.

**Carl:** Yeah! That's kind of how I've been feeling.

**Adam:** I don't know if you'd be interested, but last year I went in to see Ms. Conway, the school counselor. We talked for awhile and she helped me figure out what some of my feelings were.

**Carl:** Did you feel stupid?

**Adam:** Maybe a little at first. She didn't try telling me what to do. She mainly listened. It really helped me!

**Carl:** Maybe I would be interested. I think I'll go see her during study hall tomorrow.

**Adam:** Good! Now, how about that movie this weekend?

**Carl:** That sounds like a good idea after all. What did you say it's called?

**Adam:** I didn't. I forgot what the name of it is, but it's the one about the cop . . .

*[The two boys continue their conversation.]*

| | |
|---|---|
| **Number of Characters:** | 3 |
| **Character Description:** | Terry—A teenager |
| | David—Terry's friend |
| | Mrs. Graham—Terry's mother |
| **Scene Description:** | Terry really wants to ask Sherrie out on a date, but just can't seem to do it because he has difficulty expressing his feelings. Terry comes home from school in a bad mood because he chickened out again today. |

**Mrs. Graham:** Hi, Terry! How was school today?

*[Terry walks past his mom and into the kitchen without saying a word. Mrs. Graham follows him.]*

**Mrs. Graham:** Looks like you had a bad day. Do you want to talk about it?

**Terry:** *[Angrily]* No, I don't want to talk about it.

**Mrs. Graham:** I know it's difficult for you to express your feelings, Terry. It always has been. I know you try to work things out yourself. I hate to see you hold everything inside.

**Terry:** I really don't want to talk about it. It's no big deal. Just forget it.

*[The doorbell rings and Mrs. Graham goes to the door. It's David, Terry's best friend.]*

**David:** Hello, Mrs. Graham. Is Terry around?

**Mrs. Graham:** Hello, David. Yes, he's right in the kitchen.

*[David heads for the kitchen. Mrs. Graham hopes that Terry will open up to David.]*

**David:** Hey, Terry, how's it going?

**Terry:** OK, I guess.

**David:** Kathy and I are going to the concert this weekend. Why don't you ask someone and we'll double?

*[Terry thinks about Sherrie and how much he'd like to ask her. He remembers all over again how angry he is at himself for being too afraid to ask her.]*

**Terry:** Thanks, but no thanks. I have other plans.

**David:** Oh, come on. What other plans? The concert is going to be dynamite.

**Terry:** Look, David. If I felt like going to the concert, I'd go to the concert. If I tell you I have plans, then I have plans. You got it?

**David:** Darn right, I got it. Next time I feel like getting yelled at, I'll remember to come over here. See ya around!

*[David quickly leaves the kitchen. Mrs. Graham heard David get yelled at and catches him at the door.]*

**Mrs. Graham:** David, I'm sorry. Terry isn't mad at you at all. He's been upset about something else and won't talk about it. I knew he was going to explode. I'm sorry you were the target.

**David:** Thanks for telling me that, Mrs. Graham. I would have been trying to figure out all night exactly what I did wrong.

**Mrs. Graham:** I wish Terry was better at expressing his feelings.

**David:** I'll see you later, Mrs. Graham. Bye.

# Skill 47    Expressing Anger

**Definition of Skill:** Letting another person know, in a constructive way, about feelings of anger (Note: *Constructive* may need to be defined.)

**Skill Activities/
Discussions:**

1. Ask students to tell what makes them angry and what they do when they get angry. Using their examples, make a list of things that would help the situation, such as counting to ten, and another list of things that could make their anger worse, such as punching a school locker.

2. Encourage students to use an "I" statement when they express their anger to another person. For example, "I am feeling angry because I couldn't get what I wanted," instead of "You really make me mad because you won't let me go."

3. Compose a list of statements that people use to express their anger. Have students determine which ones are "I" statements. Have them rewrite those that are not "I" statements.

**Situations:** **Home**

You walk into your bedroom and find your brother going through your CDs without permission. You are feeling angry. Demonstrate how you would deal with your anger.

**School**

You are really angry. Your sister told your boyfriend/girlfriend that you like someone else, and it is not true. Demonstrate how you should express your anger to your sister.

**Community**

You are feeling very angry at your neighbor's son. He borrowed your bike and was reckless with it. Express your anger to him.

| | |
|---|---|
| **Number of Characters:** | 3 |
| **Character Description:** | LuAnn—A teenager |
| | Lonnie—LuAnn's brother |
| | Mrs. Stelse—LuAnn and Lonnie's mother |
| **Scene Description:** | LuAnn comes home from school and goes into her bedroom to change. Her mom is in her room, but does not hear LuAnn come in. LuAnn sees her mom looking in all her drawers and gets very angry. She counts to ten before she says anything. |

**LuAnn:** *[Angrily]* Mother, I am really angry.

**Mrs. Stelse:** About what?

**LuAnn:** Why am I angry? You're asking why I'm angry?

**Mrs. Stelse:** Yes, what are you so angry about?

*[LuAnn leaves the room and goes downstairs to the kitchen. Her brother, Lonnie, is fixing a sandwich.]*

**Lonnie:** Hi, Sis! What's wrong?

**LuAnn:** I'm really mad. I can't believe she's doing that.

**Lonnie:** Who? Mom?

**LuAnn:** Yes, Mom! She's up in my room going through all my drawers.

**Lonnie:** I don't blame you for being mad. I would be, too. Did you tell her?

**LuAnn:** No, I was too angry. I figured I better cool down first.

**Lonnie:** I think I would have just exploded at her.

**LuAnn:** Believe me, I felt like it! But it wouldn't have done any good.

*[Mrs. Stelse comes into the kitchen.]*

**Mrs. Stelse:** LuAnn, are you all right?

**LuAnn:** I'm really feeling angry because I feel like I'm not trusted when my room gets inspected. It makes me feel like you think I've done something wrong.

**Mrs. Stelse:** Oh, LuAnn! I just finished the laundry and I thought I'd put your clothes away for you. Then I started looking in your drawers to see if they needed straightening up.

**LuAnn:** Mom, we've talked about my privacy before.

**Mrs. Stelse:** I'm sorry, LuAnn. I guess I'm still treating you like a little girl. I know you can straighten your own drawers. I guess it's a hard habit to break.

**LuAnn:** I know you were just trying to help me out. Next time just leave my folded clothes in the hall. I'll put them away myself, along with my other chores.

**Mrs. Stelse:** OK, LuAnn. I get the message.

## Script B — Expressing Anger

| | |
|---|---|
| **Number of Characters:** | 4 |
| **Character Description:** | Don—A teenager |
| | Eva—A teenager |
| | Greg—A teenager |
| | Ms. Hagar—The teacher |
| **Scene Description:** | Don and Greg are sitting at a table together, eating lunch. |

**Greg:** I wonder where Eva is. She told me she would meet us here.

**Don:** Maybe Mr. Knotz held the class late. He does that when he needs more time.

**Greg:** He must think we have all the time in the world for lunch.

**Don:** Here comes Eva now.

**Eva:** Sorry I'm late. I was just talking to Mike Mitchell.

*[Eva gives Greg a dirty look.]*

**Greg:** You seem kind of upset.

**Eva:** You bet I am! You really make me mad, Greg, when you spread lies about me.

**Don:** What kind of lies? I haven't heard anything.

**Eva:** It's not important what he said!

**Greg:** Don't blame me, Eva. I didn't say anything.

**Eva:** I can't believe it! Now you're lying again. You better knock it off or you'll be sorry.

**Greg:** Calm down, Eva. Maybe we should talk about this.

**Eva:** Don't tell me to calm down! I won't calm down until you take back everything you said.

**Don:** How can he take it back unless he knows what he said?

*[Eva throws her plate of food at Don. Ms. Hagar sees what's going on and walks over to the table.]*

**Ms. Hagar:** What's going on here?

**Eva:** Nothing. I was just giving these creeps what they deserve.

**Ms. Hagar:** Eva, since you've chosen to break the rules about throwing food, you've also chosen to go to the office.

**Eva:** Listen, Ms. Hagar, this guy has been spreading lies about me. I'm not going to the office.

**Ms. Hagar:** Eva, I'm not giving you a choice. You need to go to the office.

*[Eva turns red in the face and stomps off to the office.]*

**Don:** She's got to learn how to control her temper!

**Greg:** No kidding!

## Skill 48 — Dealing with Embarrassment

**Definition of Skill:** Reacting appropriately to something that makes you feel uncomfortable and self-conscious

**Skill Activities/ Discussions:**

1. Have the students list situations that can be embarrassing.

2. Discuss a few of the situations listed in Activity #1 in greater detail. Ask students what to do or say in the situations (i.e., if they want to correct the cause, minimize their embarrassment, ignore it, distract the others, or use humor).

3. List things a person could do when embarrassed that would draw more attention to oneself and make the situation worse.

**Situations:**

**Home**
Your father sees you acting like a movie star while looking in a mirror. Demonstrate how you would deal with your embarrassment.

**School**
When you come out of the locker room, your pants are unzipped. Show how you would deal with your embarrassment.

**Community**
You spill your water when you're eating at a restaurant. Demonstrate how you would deal with your embarrassment.

| Number of Characters: | 3 |
|---|---|
| Character Description: | Amanda—A teenager |
| | Jamie—Amanda's friend |
| | Ms. Prince—The physical education teacher |
| Scene Description: | Amanda and Jamie are talking in the girls' bathroom before school. |

**Jamie:** Do you think Eric will sit with you at lunch again today?

**Amanda:** I hope not.

**Jamie:** Why? I thought you said you really like him.

**Amanda:** Oh, I do! I just don't like what I'm wearing today.

**Jamie:** Oh, come on! I like those pants. But I notice you hardly ever wear them anymore.

**Amanda:** I've outgrown them. I think I've gotten an inch and a half taller this year. Nothing else was clean this morning, so I had to wear them.

*[Jamie drops her comb. Amanda bends over to pick it up for her, and her pants rip.]*

**Jamie:** *[Giggling]* Oh, no! Now what?

**Amanda:** I can't believe this! How embarrassing! I don't want to walk down to the gym like this, Jamie. Please don't tell anyone about his.

**Jamie:** You have to admit, it is sort of funny!

**Amanda:** Yeah, I guess it is. But Jamie, if everyone finds out, it would really be embarrassing for me.

**Jamie:** OK, I won't tell. Here, why don't you tie my sweater around your waist until we get to the locker room?

| | |
|---|---|
| **Amanda:** | Thanks, Jamie! |

*[Amanda walks to the locker room and finds Ms. Prince.]*

| | |
|---|---|
| **Amanda:** | Excuse me, Ms. Prince. Could I talk to you for a minute? |
| **Ms. Prince:** | Sure, if it's only for a minute. I need to take roll call. |
| **Amanda:** | I have a big rip in my pants. Could I change into my gym uniform and then find a needle and thread to sew them up quickly? |
| **Ms. Prince:** | Do you really think that's necessary, Amanda? |
| **Amanda:** | Well the rip is pretty obvious. I just can't walk around like this all day. It would be too embarrassing. |
| **Ms. Prince:** | I see your point. Here, let me write you out a pass. Do you think there will be a sewing class going on? |
| **Amanda:** | No, I think the room is open this hour. Thank you for letting me do this. You saved my life! |

*[Ms. Prince smiles and hands Amanda the pass.]*

| **Number of Characters:** | 3 |
| --- | --- |
| **Character Description:** | Kirk—A teenager |
| | Mr. Stetson—Kirk's father |
| | Mrs. Stetson—Kirk's mother |
| **Scene Description:** | The scene begins when Kirk and his dad arrive home from Kirk's orthodontist appointment. Kirk just had braces put on. |

**Mrs. Stetson:** Hello, you two! I'm glad you're home. We only have a half-hour to eat before we go to the scout meeting. Kirk, how did it go at your orthodontist appointment?

*[Kirk doesn't say anything to his mom. He just sits down on the couch with his mouth closed.]*

**Mr. Stetson:** The doctor decided to put Kirk's braces on today instead of next week. Kirk is a little upset.

**Mrs. Stetson:** Kirk, I know how much it hurts. I can remember when I had braces at your age. The pain should go away in a few days.

**Kirk:** It's not the pain, Mom!

**Mr. Stetson:** I think Kirk is a little self-conscious.

**Kirk:** A little self-conscious, my foot! This is the most embarrassing thing that's every happened to me!

**Mrs. Stetson:** It seems like quite a few of your friends have braces, don't they?

**Mr. Stetson:** That's right! I know Craig and Germain have them, so you won't be alone.

**Kirk:** I don't care who else has them. I'm never going to show my face in public again. I know I'll get teased.

**Mr. Stetson:** I know how that goes. Seems like kids are always teasing someone for something.

**Mrs. Stetson:** This is just a suggestion, Kirk, but if kids know you are upset about their teasing, they will tease you all the more.

**Mr. Stetson:** Maybe we could think of some good responses to make when someone teases you. How about, "Girls like guys with straight teeth," or something like that?

**Kirk:** Don't waste your time, Dad. I told you I'm not going anywhere until these come off.

*[Mrs. Stetson understands that Kirk is feeling embarrassed and tries to change the subject.]*

**Mrs. Stetson:** Tell you what. Let's have lunch so we can go to the scout meeting. They are going to plan your summer camping trip today. That should be fun!

**Kirk:** I'm not going to any scout meeting!

*[The Stetsons continue their discussion.]*

© 1994 Thinking Publications
*Duplication permitted for educational use only.*

| Skill | **49** | **Coping with Fear** |

**Definition of Skill:**  Admitting that something is frightening

**Skill Activities/ Discussions:**

1. Discuss reasons why it is sometimes difficult to admit to being afraid.

2. Prepare a list of common fears and dislikes. Have students differentiate between the two.

3. Discuss why talking about fear may help to reduce it.

**Situations:**

**Home**
Your parents have asked if you would like to stay at home alone while they go out of town for the weekend. You feel uncomfortable about doing it. Discuss your fear with your parents.

**School**
You are afraid to tell the principal that you were the one who accidentally broke the front window, because of what he might do. Discuss your fear with a friend.

**Community**
You are afraid to go bowling because of the "bullies" that hang out there. Discuss your fear with someone.

| | |
|---|---|
| **Number of Characters:** | 4 |
| **Character Description:** | Tanya—A teenager |
| | Kaysie—Tanya's friend |
| | Mr. Odell—The English teacher |
| | Ms. Conway—The school counselor |
| **Scene Description:** | The scene begins when Tanya and Kaysie are in English class. |

**Mr. Odell:** Most of you have already given your oral book reports, and I must say, they have been very good. There are only a few of you we haven't heard from yet. Any volunteers who would like to give theirs tomorrow?

*[No students raise their hands.]*

**Mr. Odell:** Well, since we have no volunteers, I'll need to pick the next ones. Tanya, plan to go first tomorrow and, Kaysie, you can go after her.

*[The bell rings. Tanya and Kaysie walk out of the room together.]*

**Kaysie:** There's no way I'm getting up in front of that class tomorrow.

**Tanya:** Why, haven't you read your book yet?

**Kaysie:** Oh, I've read it all right. I'm just afraid of making a fool of myself.

**Tanya:** Me, too! I'm glad I'm not the only one who feels that way.

**Kaysie:** Well, I've decided I'm not going to do it. I'd rather take an "F" on the unit.

**Tanya:** I've thought about that too, but I just can't afford an "F." I didn't do very well on the last test.

**Kaysie:** I'll talk to you tomorrow. I've got to catch the bus.

**Tanya:** Bye, Kaysie.

*[Tanya thinks about her fear of getting up in front of the class some more. She decides to go talk to the guidance counselor about it.]*

**Tanya:** Excuse me, Ms. Conway. Do you have a minute to talk?

**Ms. Conway:** I sure do, Tanya! What's on your mind?

**Tanya:** I have to give an oral book report tomorrow in English. I feel really stupid! I just don't think I can go through with it. Almost everyone else has given theirs.

**Ms. Conway:** It sounds like you're nervous about getting up in front of the class.

**Tanya:** I must be really weird. I shouldn't be afraid to give a book report to my friends.

**Ms. Conway:** Tanya, did you know that the number one fear that adults have is public speaking?

**Tanya:** Really?

**Ms. Conway:** Yes! And most people say it's harder when you know your audience personally.

**Tanya:** Then, I'm not weird, am I?

**Ms. Conway:** I can guarantee you that the more times you speak to an audience, the easier it gets. I've also heard that it's good to be a little nervous, because then your body is prepared to be more alert.

**Tanya:** Really? Well, I'm still afraid about tomorrow.

**Ms. Conway:** Tanya, what's the worst thing that could happen?

**Tanya:** I could forget what I want to say and get laughed at.

**Ms. Conway:** Did anyone else forget when they gave theirs?

**Tanya:** Sure. Steve and May both did.

**Ms. Conway:** Did they get laughed at?

**Tanya:** Yeah, a little. The teacher just let them try again the next day. You know, when I look at it that way, I guess it doesn't seem all that bad. I wouldn't be the only one to forget my report.

**Ms. Conway:** Just remember, it's normal to feel nervous.

*[Tanya and Ms. Conway continue to talk.]*

## Script B — Coping with Fear

| | |
|---|---|
| **Number of Characters:** | 3 |
| **Character Description:** | Kyle—A teenager |
| | Sue—A teenager |
| | Ms. Baymer—The boss |
| **Scene Description:** | Kyle and Sue work at clearing tables in a local restaurant. The scene begins when they are folding napkins for the night, before the restaurant opens up. |

**Ms. Baymer:** Say, Kyle. The restaurant opens in 15 minutes. The waitresses need more glasses. I'd like you to go down in the basement and bring up a few boxes of them.

**Kyle:** Why me?

**Ms. Baymer:** Because I asked you to.

*[Kyle has been in the basement before. It doesn't have many lights and he is uncomfortable going down there alone again.]*

**Sue:** Am I ever glad she asked you and not me. That basement gives me the creeps.

*[Kyle doesn't want to admit that he is afraid, too.]*

**Kyle:** Are you serious? What are you afraid of? The boogy man?

**Sue:** No! It just gives me the creeps. That's all. You'd better move it. Ms. Baymer is waiting.

**Kyle:** She can wait all night. I'm not getting the glasses.

**Sue:** Do you want someone to go with you? Maybe you're afraid too but just won't admit it.

**Kyle:** No, I don't want someone to go with me! I'm not going because it's not my job. If the waitresses need the glasses, then let them go into the basement and get them.

**Sue:** But the boss asked you to!

**Kyle:** I've got better things to do, like fold these napkins.

> *[Ms. Baymer looks at Kyle and wonders why he hasn't gone down for the glasses yet. Kyle doesn't want to make her mad, but he also doesn't want to admit he is afraid.]*

**Ms. Baymer:** Kyle, I thought I asked you to get the glasses. Would you like someone to go with you?

**Kyle:** No, I don't need someone to go with me. I'm not going because it's not my job.

**Ms. Baymer:** Kyle, I'd like to see you in my office before you leave tonight.

**Kyle:** Yes, ma'am.

| Skill | **50** | Expressing "Safe" Humor |

**Definition of Skill:** Saying something funny that is not at anyone's expense; something that everyone can laugh at

**Skill Activities/ Discussions:**

1. Discuss the difference between "safe" humor and "unsafe" humor. Have the students think of examples of both.

2. Ask students how they feel about someone who is always joking around and can never be serious.

3. Discuss the positive aspects of humor (e.g., reduction of stress).

4. Discuss the idea that when you tease someone, it should not be about a sensitive weakness.

**Situations:**

**Home**
It's April Fools' Day. Demonstrate a safe joke to play on your dad.

**School**
You're at school. Demonstrate a safe joke you could tell to your teacher.

**Community**
You deliver papers. Demonstrate safe humor you could express to your boss.

| | |
|---|---|
| **Number of Characters:** | 3 |
| **Character Description:** | Bonnie—A teenager |
| | Lee—Bonnie's friend |
| | Mr. King—Bonnie's father |
| **Scene Description:** | When Bonnie gets home from school, she goes out to the back yard to find her dad. |

**Mr. King:** Hi, Bonnie! How was school today?

**Bonnie:** Great! How was your day?

**Mr. King:** It was fine. I decided to come home early. I wanted to get started on the lawn work.

**Bonnie:** Do you need any help?

**Mr. King:** First you say school was great and then you ask if I need any help?

**Bonnie:** Yeah! What's wrong with that?

**Mr. King:** Nothing! Don't get me wrong! I'm not complaining. *[In a teasing tone of voice]* You've been in such a good mood lately. It must be Lee! I suppose he's coming over again today, right?

**Bonnie:** Oh, Dad! Give me a break.

**Mr. King:** I don't mind. I really like him. He's got a good sense of humor.

**Bonnie:** He really does. He's always making me laugh.

**Mr. King:** It feels good to laugh, doesn't it?

**Bonnie:** Yeah, it does! Lee never makes jokes that hurt other people's feelings though, like Craig Palmer does.

**Mr. King:** I think I know the type.

**Bonnie:** He doesn't joke around too much either. He does have his serious moments.

**Mr. King:** *[Teasing Bonnie again]* You say he gets serious, ha?

**Bonnie:** Knock it off, Dad! You know what I mean.

**Mr. King:** Oh, come on! I'm just teasing you. Why don't you invite him over for dinner tonight?

**Bonnie:** OK! I'll go call him.

*[Bonnie goes into the house to call Lee. An hour later, Lee arrives for dinner. Everyone is seated at the table.]*

**Mr. King:** I'm glad you could make it for dinner tonight, Lee.

**Lee:** Believe me, I'm really glad Bonnie called and invited me! My parents are at a meeting tonight. I was going to have to cook my own supper. Considering the way I cook, I probably would have ended up at the hospital!

*[Everyone at the table chuckles.]*

**Mr. King:** Lee, I really like your sense of humor.

**Lee:** Thank you, Mr. King, I like to make people laugh.

*[Lee, Bonnie, and Mr. King continue eating.]*

| | |
|---|---|
| **Number of Characters:** | 4 |
| **Character Description:** | Sarah—A teenager |
| | Chad—A teenager |
| | Mike—A teenager |
| | Mr. Sorensen—The teacher |
| **Scene Description:** | Sarah, Chad, and Mike are all in English class. The scene begins when Mr. Sorensen starts the class. |

**Mr. Sorensen:** Today, I'd like us to begin reading the play "Romeo and Juliet." I'd like to have volunteers to read the parts.

**Chad:** Could I read Friar Lawrence's part?

**Mr. Sorensen:** That would be fine. Thank you for volunteering. Anyone else?

*[No students raise their hands.]*

**Mr. Sorensen:** Sarah, how would you like to read the part for Juliet?

**Sarah:** That all depends on if I have to kiss Romeo or not.

*[Everyone, including Mr. Sorensen, laughs at Sarah's humor.]*

**Mr. Sorensen:** You're safe, Sarah! No kissing in this play.

**Sarah:** OK, I'll take the part.

**Mr. Sorensen:** Mike, I'd like you to read the part of Romeo, OK?

**Mike:** Sure.

**Mr. Sorensen:** For those of you who do not have a part to read, please listen carefully and follow along. Tomorrow, I will have different readers, so you'll all get a chance.

*[Sarah lets out a loud burp and the kids in class laugh again. Mr. Sorensen gives her a stern look.]*

**Chad:** *[Whispering to Sarah]* You're quite the comic today, Sarah!

**Sarah:** I thought this class needed a little spicing up!

**Mr. Sorensen:** Sarah, would you please begin reading?

**Sarah:** Yes, sir!

*[Sarah burps again, hoping to make the kids laugh. No one laughs anymore.]*

**Mr. Sorensen:** Sarah, enough is enough. Please read!

**Sarah:** Now, what part do I have? Romeo or Juliet?

**Mike:** Come on, Sarah. You're not funny anymore. Just read, OK?

**Chad:** Let's get going, Sarah. I want to get a chance to start my homework. At this rate, we will have to read until the end of the hour.

**Mr. Sorensen:** Sarah, I'm afraid I'll have to pick another Juliet. Please see me after class.

*[Sarah can't figure out why everybody is so serious all of a sudden.]*

# Skill 51    Accepting "Safe" Humor

**Definition of Skill:**    When being teased in an appropriate way, laughing along with the joke

**Skill Activities/
Discussions:**

1. Ask students how they feel about someone who is always serious and never laughs.

2. Ask students to tell about times when they have been teased in an appropriate way and times they have been teased in an inappropriate way.

3. Discuss the importance of humor in people's lives.

**Situations:**    **Home**

In the morning, you asked your mom, "What's for dinner tonight?" She replied, "Your favorite, liver and onions, with spinach." You do not like liver and spinach. All day long, you thought about how you could avoid eating dinner. At dinner time, you were the last one to the table. Everyone said, "Surprise!" Your mom had made your favorite dinner. The family started laughing. Laugh with your family.

**School**

You stopped with a group of friends at the fountain for a drink. When you pushed the fountain button, there was barely any water. The second time you pushed the button, you put your face really close to get a drink. This time, the water streamed up and got your face wet. The kids started laughing. You remarked, "I needed my face washed anyway!" Laugh along with them, while you dry your face off.

**Community**

You are with friends at a restaurant. You order a hamburger. When it comes, you open the bun to put on more ketchup. When you look inside there is no meat. Your friends start laughing. You say something about needing to lose weight anyway. Laugh with your friends.

| Number of Characters: | 3 |
|---|---|
| **Character Description:** | José—A teenager |
| | Rosa—A teenager |
| | Carlos—A teenager |
| **Scene Description:** | José and Rosa have history class together. The teacher passes back their tests during class. The scene begins when the bell rings and the two of them walk out of class together. |

**Rosa:** How did you do on the test, José? I remember you said you studied pretty hard for it.

**José:** Yeah, I did! I guess the studying paid off. I got an "A-."

**Rosa:** That's great! Way to go! You always get such good grades. I wish I had the self-discipline to study as much as you do.

**José:** People tease me about being so smart. Sometimes I'm not sure they realize how much work it takes to get good grades.

*[Rosa and José join Carlos at one of the lunch tables in the cafeteria.]*

**Carlos:** Hi, you two! How's it going?

**José:** Not bad.

**Rosa:** Hi Carlos!

**Carlos:** You two just had Mr. Brunsell for history, right?

**José:** Right. Why?

**Carlos:** Did he pass back the tests today? I have him after lunch.

**José:** Yeah! You'll get it back at the end of the hour.

**Carlos:** So, how did you both do?

**Rosa:**   *[Smiling]* Oh, I did OK. It's José who didn't do so well.

*[Carlos catches on to Rosa's humor.]*

**Carlos:**   Failed another one, José? You know, you really should start studying more.

*[Carlos and Rosa start to laugh. José knows they are teasing him in a nice way, so he laughs along.]*

**José:**   You're right, Carlos! I should. I just don't seem to have much interest.

**Rosa:**   No, seriously, Carlos. José studied hard and did quite well. I'm really proud of him.

**Carlos:**   That's great, José! Now, I want you both to keep your fingers crossed for me!

| | |
|---|---|
| **Number of Characters:** | 4 |
| **Character Description:** | Melissa—A teenager |
| | Mrs. Brock—Melissa's mother |
| | Mr. Brock—Melissa's father |
| | Frank—The door person |
| **Scene Description:** | The Brock family has heard about a fun, new restaurant that opened up downtown. They decide to go out to eat there. The scene begins when they are just arriving at the restaurant. |

**Mr. Brock:** Well, you two, be prepared for a fun evening. I hear this place is really wild!

**Mrs. Brock:** Do you know anyone else who's been there yet?

**Mr. Brock:** The Lehmers went last weekend and loved it! They wouldn't tell me anything specific about it because they said they didn't want to spoil any of the surprises.

**Melissa:** I can't wait to see the inside of this place. It sounds great!

*[The front door to the restaurant has a sign on it that says "OPEN." When Mr. Brock tries to open the door, it feels like it's locked. A small window in the door opens and all they can see is a pair of eyes.]*

**Frank:** What's the password?

**Mrs. Brock:** *[Laughing]* Well, I don't know.

**Frank:** That's it! Come on in.

*[The Brocks start to laugh as the front door opens. They walk into the restaurant and the hostess shows them to their table. They soon find out that there are singing waiters and waitresses.]*

| | |
|---|---|
| **Melissa:** | I think I'm going to run to the bathroom. Do you see a sign anywhere? |
| **Mr. Brock:** | Look at the top of that big staircase. The sign says "LADIES POWDER ROOM." That must be it. |
| **Melissa:** | Thanks, Dad. I'll be right back. I don't want to miss anything. |

*[Melissa walks halfway up the staircase and notices that one of the steps is a different color. As soon as she steps on it, lights start flashing, and bells start ringing. Everyone in the restaurant looks up at Melissa and starts to laugh. Melissa gets upset and runs down the steps and back out to the car.]*

| | |
|---|---|
| **Mrs. Brock:** | I bet those bells go off every time some woman goes up those stairs. I can't believe Melissa didn't figure out it was one of the pranks, just like the front door. |
| **Mr. Brock:** | I'll go outside and get her. |

*[Mr. Brock follows Melissa out to the parking lot.]*

| | |
|---|---|
| **Mr. Brock:** | Melissa, don't get upset! It was just one of their pranks. You'll hear those bells go off all night, whenever a lady goes to the bathroom. I think you were just startled. |
| **Melissa:** | I wasn't startled. I was humiliated! I'm not going back in there. |
| **Mr. Brock:** | Oh, Melissa! They weren't laughing at you. They were laughing at the prank. You just happened to be the one on the step at that time. |
| **Melissa:** | I'm not going back in there. I'll stay out in the car until you and Mom are finished. |
| **Mr. Brock:** | I'm sorry you feel that way, Melissa! If you change your mind, please come back in. |

---

# Skill 52 — Dealing with Failure

**Definition of Skill:** Deciding why an activity was not successful and whether to try the desired activity again

**Skill Activities/ Discussions:**

1. Ask students what the following phrase means: *If at first you don't succeed, try, try again.*

2. Discuss the idea that occasionally people may choose not to try again, but rather, to try something else. For example, they decide they were not meant to sing, so they decide to learn an instrument instead.

3. Discuss the feelings that can be associated with failure.

**Situations:**

**Home**
You always lose when you play a board game with your older brother. Demonstrate how you would respond to that failure.

**School**
You fail a test at school. Show how you respond.

**Community**
Your team comes in last place in the city baseball league. Show how you should deal with that failure.

## Script **A** — Dealing with Failure

| | |
|---|---|
| **Number of Characters:** | 4 |
| **Character Description:** | Katrina—A teenager |
| | Jessica—Katrina's friend |
| | Coach Simon—The volleyball coach |
| | Brenda—A teenager |
| **Scene Description:** | Katrina is trying out for the volleyball team. The scene begins when Coach Simon announces who made the team. |

**Coach Simon:** I want to thank you all for trying out for the volleyball team this year. You've all worked very hard the past two weeks at practice. As you know, I can only accept 16 of you for the varsity and junior varsity teams. I have chosen the teams and will read the names of the girls I have chosen. Brenda Dasler, Sue Landowski, . . .

*[Katrina does not hear her name called and knows that means she did not make either of the teams. She notices that Brenda, who did make the varsity team, is sitting right next to her.]*

**Katrina:** Brenda, congratulations! I'm happy that you made the team.

**Brenda:** Thanks, Katrina. I'm sorry you didn't make it.

**Katrina:** You can't win them all.

*[Katrina changes clothes and walks home. Her good friend, Jessica, happens to be leaving the school at the same time.]*

**Jessica:** Hi, Katrina!

**Katrina:** Hi, Jesse! What are you doing here so late?

**Jessica:** I was making up some work for Mr. Sudow from when I was sick. How about you?

**Katrina:** I was at volleyball practice.

**Jessica:** Oh, that's right. I forgot. Hey, weren't you guys going to find out who made the teams today?

**Katrina:** Yeah, we did. Only I didn't make either one.

**Jessica:** Oh, Katrina, I'm sorry. I know you were really counting on it.

**Katrina:** I'm pretty disappointed. I really like volleyball.

**Jessica:** I don't know why you didn't make it. It can't be because you didn't try hard enough.

**Katrina:** I'm pretty sure it's because of my serving. I'm fine at bumping and setting. I just can't seem to get my serve right.

**Jessica:** Is there anything you can do about that?

**Katrina:** I can really concentrate on my serves and practice a lot this summer.

**Jessica:** That sounds like a good plan. Are you going to try out again next year?

**Katrina:** I don't know. I have to decide if I want to go out for volleyball again or try something different. I'll have to think about it.

*[The two girls continue walking home.]*

| | |
|---|---|
| **Number of Characters:** | 3 |
| **Character Description:** | Luke—A teenager |
| | Parker—Luke's older brother |
| | Ms. Smith—Luke and Parker's mother |
| **Scene Description:** | The scene begins when the Smiths are having dinner. |

**Parker:** Luke, I hear your science teacher is giving a big test tomorrow. Some of the kids were talking about it after school today.

*[Luke gives Parker a look that says, "Why did you have to mention that?"]*

**Ms.Smith:** It's interesting that you should bring that up. Luke, guess who called me after school today?

**Luke:** Who?

**Ms.Smith:** Your science teacher. He is very concerned about your grade and said you failed the first test. He also said you haven't done many of the assignments from the last unit. He wanted me to encourage you to study for the test tonight.

**Luke:** Study! Why should I study? It won't do me any good anyway.

**Parker:** Oh, come on, Luke. I always do better on a test when I study for it.

**Luke:** Oh, yeah? Well, I studied for the first test and got an "F," so I told myself to forget it.

**Ms.Smith:** Luke, when you fail at something, don't just give up! Try to figure out why you failed, and then try it differently the next time.

**Luke:** How am I supposed to do that?

**Parker:** Maybe it's not the fact that you studied that made you fail, but how you studied.

**Luke:** What's wrong with the way I studied? I read the chapter the night before I take the test. Isn't that how everybody studies?

**Parker:** Everybody has to find a way to study that works best for them. I don't have any work tonight. Would you like me to show you how I study for a test? Maybe it will work for you too.

**Luke:** Sure, I'll give it another shot.

_[The boys head to their room to get started._
_Ms. Smith checks in on them much later.]_

**Ms.Smith:** Well, guys, how is the studying going?

**Parker:** Luke has really been working hard.

**Luke:** Parker has shown me a lot of good ways to study. I'm going to do great on this test.

**Parker:** I know you'll do much better than you would have if you hadn't studied. I am concerned though. I forgot that Luke hadn't done any work this unit. We aren't as far as we should be, but I'm beat.

**Ms.Smith:** That is something to keep in mind, Luke. You may not see a big increase in your grade. It's difficult to cram for a test all in one night.

**Parker:** That's true. But, if you keep up the good work all during the next unit, I'm sure you'll do well on the next test.

**Luke:** No problem. I've never studied this hard in my life. I know I'll get a good grade on this test tomorrow!

_[The next day at school, Luke takes the test. Later, he_
_finds out that he got another F. When the test is_
_handed back, he crumples it up and throws it away.]_

**Luke:** I knew it. I never should have studied for this test. It's hopeless. I'll never study again.

---

## Skill 53    Expressing Affection

**Definition of Skill:**    Letting another person know about good feelings

**Skill Activities/ Discussions:**

1. Help students brainstorm a list of people to whom they might express their affection (e.g., a close friend, parent, brother, sister, boyfriend, girlfriend). Help them to draw the conclusion that expressing affection does not have to be tied to romance.

2. Discuss the idea that people can express their affection by telling another person how they feel or by doing something.

3. List possible actions that would express affection (e.g., giving a card, a gift, a hug).

**Situations:**

**Home**

It is Father's Day and you want to let your father know how much he means to you. Demonstrate how you would express your affection for him.

**School**

It is the last day of school and your best friend is leaving for the summer. Express your affection to your friend.

**Community**

You have made good friends with an elderly couple in your neighborhood and enjoy spending time at their house. Demonstrate how you would express your affection for them.

# Script A Expressing Affection

| | |
|---|---|
| **Number of Characters:** | 3 |
| **Character Description:** | Doug—A teenager |
| | Molly—Doug's older sister |
| | Mr. Long—Doug and Molly's father |
| **Scene Description:** | Molly is going away to school and will be leaving soon. Mr. Long and Doug planned a big surprise party for her. The scene begins when the party has just ended. |

**Molly:** I can't believe you two planned that party without my knowing it. When did you get everything ready?

**Mr. Long:** It wasn't easy, but Doug and I can be pretty sneaky when we want to be. Can't we, Doug?

**Doug:** Yup! Remember a couple weeks ago when you were giving me such a hard time about talking to Jeff so much on the phone?

**Molly:** I sure do! I had a call to make and every time I went to dial, you were on the phone.

**Doug:** *[Laughing]* I wasn't talking to Jeff at all! I was calling to invite everyone to your party. When you would come into the room, I just pretended I was talking to him.

**Molly:** You sneak! I suppose that was a setup with Grandma this morning, too?

**Mr. Long:** We told her to call you and ask you to go over to her house so we could get everything ready here for the party.

**Molly:** You two are something else! I really appreciate your doing that for me. I've never been so surprised in my entire life!

**Mr. Long:** I'm glad you enjoyed it, Molly. I better get Grandma's chairs back to her.

**Doug:** We'll start picking up around here while you're gone.

| | |
|---|---|
| **Mr. Long:** | I won't be gone long. Bye. |
| **Molly:** | Bye. |
| **Doug:** | Maybe we should have one more piece of cake before we start. |
| **Molly:** | I can't! I'm stuffed. |
| **Doug:** | I see you've started packing for school already. |
| **Molly:** | I've only got four more days before I leave. |
| **Doug:** | All right! Only four more days until I have the bathroom and stereo all to myself. |
| **Molly:** | Very funny! |
| **Doug:** | Seriously, Molly, I can't believe you're leaving. It won't be the same around here. |
| **Molly:** | I'm going to miss you and Dad! |
| **Doug:** | We'll miss you, too! You know, Molly, I haven't told you this before, but I'm really glad you're my sister. |
| **Molly:** | Thanks, Doug. That really means a lot to me. |
| **Doug:** | Enough of this mushy stuff. We better get started on this mess. |
| **Molly:** | Wow! Just look at these dishes! |

*[They decide to start with the kitchen first.]*

| | |
|---|---|
| **Number of Characters:** | 2 |
| **Character Description:** | Brandon—A teenager |
| | Mr. Kent—Brandon's father |
| **Scene Description:** | The scene begins when Brandon and his father are fishing together. |

**Brandon:** What kind of fishing lure are you gonna use, Dad?

**Mr. Kent:** I think I'll start with a Rapala. How about you?

**Brandon:** I'm going to give this Red Devil a try. Come on, fish! I hope you're out there today.

**Mr. Kent:** What do you and the guys have planned for this weekend?

**Brandon:** Nothing, I guess. Mark and Steve have plans, so I thought I'd stick around home.

**Mr. Kent:** Oh, yeah? What are they going to be up to?

**Brandon:** They both have dates for the homecoming dance on Saturday night.

**Mr. Kent:** Now that you mention it, I thought you'd probably be going, too.

**Brandon:** I was thinking about asking Ruth.

**Mr. Kent:** She's the girl you walk home from school with sometimes, isn't she?

**Brandon:** Yeah. She's really nice.

**Mr. Kent:** It's too bad she couldn't go. You would have had a nice time.

**Brandon:** I never asked her. When you ask a girl to a dance, then she knows you like her.

**Mr. Kent:** That's true. Don't you like her?

**Brandon:** I do like her, Dad! I just have a really hard time trying to tell her.

**Mr. Kent:** Sometimes it's difficult expressing your affection for somebody. But once you do it, you find out it's not so bad. Is she going to the dance with someone else?

**Brandon:** No. I know she really wants to go. I think she was hoping I'd ask her.

**Mr. Kent:** Well, it's not too late! You could still ask!

**Brandon:** I've tried, Dad. I just can't do it.

**Mr. Kent:** Those dances can be a lot of fun, Brandon. I hate to see you miss out on it, especially when there is someone you'd like to ask. Why don't you give it another try?

**Brandon:** Well, I'm not going to ask, so you can just forget it.

**Mr. Kent:** OK! Subject closed. Have you gotten any bites yet on that Red Devil?

*[Brandon is angry at himself because he has*
*a hard time expressing his affection.]*